TEXAS TOUGH

Dangerous Men in Dangerous Times

By

Gra'Delle Duncan

Illustrated By Don Moore

EAKIN PRESS Fort Worth, Texas
www.EakinPress.com

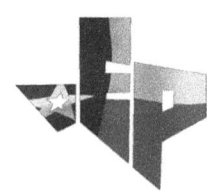

Copyright © 1990
By Gra'Delle Duncan
Published By Eakin Press
An Imprint of Wild Horse Media Group
P.O. Box 331779
Fort Worth, Texas 76163
1-817-344-7036
www.EakinPress.com
ALL RIGHTS RESERVED
1 2 3 4 5 6 7 8 9
Paperback ISBN 978-1-68179-242-2
Hardback ISBN 978-0-89015-697-1
eBook ISBN 978-1-68179-307-8

ALL RIGHTS RESERVED. No part of this book may be reproduced in any form without written permission from the publisher, except for brief passages included in a review appearing in a newspaper or magazine.

Contents

Preface	v
Moment of Truth	1

    The Battle of San Jacinto climaxing the Texas Revolution was more like a slaughter than battle. All the frustrations of delayed fighting and hatred against the Mexicans broke loose and resulted in a maddened free-for-all.

Indian Fighter	9

    On a dangerous frontier where every man either had steady nerves or perished, John Coffee "Jack" Hays amazed his fellow men.

A Bloody Mess	17

    The Council House Fight in San Antonio, March 19, 1840, hit an all-time low in diplomacy and destroyed any future friendly relationships between the Republic of Texas and the Comanches.

Sweet Revenge	23

    The War of 1846 gave Texans a welcomed opportunity to get even with the Mexicans, not only for the Alamo and Goliad killings but for the later Dawson Massacre and ill treatment of Texas prisoners taken in the Santa Fe and Mier expeditions.

Captive Luck	31

    Courage and toughness were not always enough to save a life on the Texas frontier; sometimes it required a lot of luck. In 1855, an alarm watch made the difference for one Indian captive.

Home Front Atrocities	37

    During the Civil War, Union sympathizers (anyone who had voted to keep Texas in the Union) were subjected to widespread harassment, robbery, and murder throughout the state.

Heel-Flies   45
    The kids who served in the Home Guard during the Civil War made life miserable for just about anyone they could.

Vengeance   53
    Two brothers waged a vendetta against vigilantes who lynched their father.

Two of a Kind   59
    When Texas was overrun with outlaws following the Civil War, two of the most typical to reach fame or infamy were John Wesley Hardin and Bill Longley.

Vigilantes   65
    When outlaws took over Texas in the 1870s, vigilantes fought back with no-holds-barred.

Fightin' Family   73
    Feuding, fussing, and fighting was a way of life for the Horrells of Lampasas. Before the brothers were done, they had raised havoc in both Texas and New Mexico.

Empty Saddles   79
    McNelly's Rangers cleaned up the Nueces Strip the hard way, when others — playing by the rules — had failed.

Another "Kid"   85
    Scott Cooley, who made the Mason County War his own fight, was as near to being a Texas version of Billy the Kid as makes no difference.

Pepper Hot Salt War   93
    The El Paso Salt War hit an all-time low in skullduggery as both Anglos and Mexicans fought each other to be the ones to shake down the poor salt merchants.

Female of the Species   101
    Bell Starr, tough as any man, was so obsessed with her own image as "Queen of the Outlaws" she didn't realize when she'd made a fatal mistake.

Bibliography   107

Preface

Touchy and tough, Texans have always been inflammable — but never more dangerous than in the nineteenth century. During these turbulent times, Texans forged a unique character for themselves — tough and strong — and created the Texas mystique.

Pure, undiluted hatred vied with unbelievable courage. Raw cruelty, callousness, and meanness went hand-in-hand with loyalty, trust, and affection.

Such contrasts lick like flames up through the pages of nineteenth-century Texas literature, leaving behind many a half-told tale.

Through the eyes of those who were there, or were close enough as makes no difference, one can glimpse what it might really have been like.

Presented here is a bit of the essence and flavoring often left out of the historical account.

When the bugle finally blew behind the Mexican lines, Col. Pedro Delgado stood on ammunition boxes ("the better to observe the movements of the enemy") and was later able to describe the attacking Texians while they were still in formation, seconds before the slaughter commenced.

Moment of Truth

Not a battle, not a fight, just pure slaughter marked the so-called Battle of San Jacinto, April 21, 1836, famous climax to the Texas Revolution.

Lasting officially only eighteen to twenty minutes (the length of time it took the Texans to win it), the killing went on until sundown.

Some 750 Texans whipped the hell out of more than 1,290 Mexicans, killing at least 600 and taking another 650 prisoner (some forty escaped). Two Texans died on the battlefield and six later from wounds.

San Jacinto was not only the deciding battle of the Texas Revolution, it was the first real chance the Texans had been given to even the score after the Mexican army wiped out the defenders of the Alamo, and their massacre of the Texian prisoners being held at Goliad.

For those ragged, disgruntled, near mutinous Texas troops it was "the moment of truth." They moved in for the kill with burning rage, simmering near the boiling point after six weeks of despised retreat before the enemy.

All efforts by the Mexicans to surrender were ignored, and their attempts to escape into the brush were blocked as far as possible.

As early as Gonzales, where the retreat started March 13, Sam Houston, commanding the Texas army, knew the fate of the revolution would be decided on the outcome of one battle. To choose the right moment and right place for this battle, he drove the men who stuck with him — as most of them did — at an exhausting pace along muddy roads in almost unrelenting rain.

"His temper — always volatile — was not easy, and time and again he unleashed blistering curses," recalled one of the men.

Trooper J. H. Kuykendall was particularly incensed, as were other Texans, when Houston ordered most of the men to leave their mounts behind and travel afoot. The general wanted only a small cavalry detachment.

At that point many men went home, but Kuykendall pointed out in later writings, "those that stayed showed great patriotism as a horse was considered a necessity of life."

Most of the volunteer rebels wanted to find the Mexicans and fight; retreat was something the men could hardly put up with. Some, of course, didn't and left. But new recruits were arriving almost daily from the States. One group from Cincinnati brought the army a gift of two cannons, promptly dubbed by the men as "the Two Sisters."

To the surprise of the Mexican general (and president of Mexico) Santa Anna, Houston's ragtag army was first to reach Lynch's Ferry on the San Jacinto River, where the Mexican leader had intended to waylay them.

But, by the time Santa Anna arrived with his troops, Houston had already crossed and was neatly established in a screen of trees in the fork of Buffalo Bayou and the San Jacinto River. His position fronted on the mile-long, knee-high grassy plain about to become the battlefield. Later that night, reinforcements arrived for Santa Anna and he had all of them throw up breastworks for the battle he expected to start at daylight.

The Texas troopers were also expecting orders to attack in the morning. It seemed to everyone but Houston the logical time to start a fight when both sides were lined up waiting. By noon, when no orders came for the attack, the exhausted Mexicans were ready for a nap and the Texans were boiling mad and on the verge of mutiny.

While later historians had no problem attributing the win in spite of overwhelming odds to the genius of Houston, this certainly wasn't the case at the time among either officers or men.

One of his officers, Capt. Moseley Baker, later wrote Houston a scathing letter in which he said just what he and the others felt about the whole campaign from Gonzales to San Jacinto. Noting how Houston avoided every opportunity to fight, he said in part: "You were an object of hatred and disgust, and the proposition was entertained to arrest you for the future disposition of the cabinet." But he admits no one had the guts to do it.

Houston certainly had pushed his luck in trying to hold the men back from fighting, and may have given the word to form up just in time. During the morning, Baker told Houston, "various members of the army were seen publicly and fearlessly going from company to company soliciting volunteers to fight the enemy without your consent."

Finally, at 3:30 P.M., says a later writer, "the Texians ready, rested and fed, their weapons primed, every nerve on edge" finally got their long-awaited orders. They took their positions in a double line under a bright sun with a light breeze blowing. Each man was separated by two or more yards, the line stretching some 900 yards in front of the woods.

With cannon shielding the drummer and fifers, and cavalry bringing up one end of the line, the battle array would have been an interesting sight to any Mexican sentry posted. None apparently was.

"We marched upon the enemy with the stillness of death," recalled one participant, John S. Menefee.

When 200 yards short of the Mexican barricades (behind which most of the Mexicans slept, their arms stacked), Houston gave the command to attack.

That was the last command to be obeyed by the charging Texians. With it came the roll of the drum and the shrilling fifes playing the most inappropriate tune ever to spur on a desperate, maddened army to victory — "Come To The Bower." This drinking and bawdy-house ballad was the only tune all the fifers knew.

The words, known by nearly all the troopers were:

> *Will you come to the bow'r I have shaded for you?*
> *Our bed shall be roses all spangled with dew*
> *There under the bow'r on roses you'll lie*
> *A blush on your cheek but a smile in your eye.*

A bugle finally sounded behind the Mexican lines. But, for nearly half of them, it was too late.

A Mexican officer, Col. Pedro Delgado, who survived to be captured, later described the sight of the advancing Texans: "I stepped upon some ammunition boxes, the better to observe the movements of the enemy. I saw that their formation was a mere line of one rank, and very extended. In their center was the Texas flag; on both wings they had two light cannons, well manned. Their cavalry was opposite our front, overlapping our left. In this disposition, yelling furiously, with a brisk fire of grape, muskets and rifles, they advanced resolutely upon our camp. There the utmost confusion prevailed."

Delgado must have been pretty cool to observe all these details (even if not exact on a few of them). However, the Mexican officer certainly knew what happened on his side of the barricade: "The Texans pursued the Mexicans in all directions, shooting them down or clubbing them with their guns, for they had no bayonets . . . 'Remember the Alamo! Remember Goliad' Texans shouted again and again as they pursued the panic-stricken Mexicans. When the purport of these words dawned upon the bewildered senses of the Mexican soldiers, they began to beg for mercy, and to cry out 'Me no Alamo! Me no Goliad!' But during the conflict . . . no quarter was given."

Mexican fatalities, in addition to the ranks, included one general, four colonels, two lieutenant colonels, five captains, and twelve lieutenants.

But official reports filed later by the Texans, outlining precisely the assignment of each company, would lead anyone reading them to believe the battle went off in fine style. In actual fact, the Texans ran amok.

With shouts and blood-curdling yells, they were out to avenge friends, relatives, and others slain by the Mexicans. The Texans killed without mercy in a frenzy of hatred.

Houston, having had two horses shot out from under him, tried to pull things together despite a very painfully shattered ankle. He was horrified at the lack of discipline. While his troops ran riot, he knew, as he wrote later, that they could be wiped out by a hundred well-trained soldiers. And there was still a large Mexican force unaccounted for in Texas.

Another of Houston's officers, Capt. Amasa Turner, felt much as Baker. Not realizing why Houston was attempting to halt the needless killing and bring some order out of the chaos, he later reported he heard Houston call out, "All is lost, all is lost; my God, all is lost."

Receiving little sympathy from his staff who gathered around him, Houston then exclaimed, "Have I a friend in this world? Col. Wharton, I am wounded, I am wounded, have I a friend in this world?"

At the moment, he apparently had very few.

Noah Smithwick, detailed elsewhere during the battle, arrived too late to participate, much to his disgust. In his book *The Evolution of a State,* he described the scene following the battle: "... dead Mexicans lay in piles, the survivors not even asking permission to bury them, thinking, perhaps that in return for the butchery they had practiced they would soon be lying dead themselves ...

"The battlefield bore testimony to the desperate hand-to-hand struggle our men had maintained — rifles broken off at the breach, the stocks besmeared with blood and brains told too plainly how the foe had met their death."

Smithwick also expressed regret that as a nonparticipant he received "no shares of the spoils, which were quite considerable."

Knowing that his victorious army remained very vulnerable if the fresh Mexican troops still in Texas arrived, Houston sweated it out until Santa Anna himself was captured, which wasn't until the next morning.

Fortunately, Santa Anna's captors didn't recognize him (he was disguised as a common soldier) and brought him in alive. Even then, the Texans were for gutting him on the spot when the other Mexican prisoners blew his cover by hailing him with *"El Presidente, El Presidente!"* But, by then the Texas officers could control their men.

As soon as Santa Anna was captured, Houston knew he had his ace-in-the-hole. The Mexican troops still loose in Texas would not attack while their leader was a prisoner.

The Texans had not only won the battle, they had won the war. And, except for a few of his subordinates who got their frustrations off their chests in letters and memoirs, Houston came out "Hero of San Jacinto."

Unfortunately, the hatred, distrust, and brutality engendered on both sides during the Texas Revolution, culminating at San Jacinto, set the tone for all future relationships between Mexicans and Texans, surviving at least until modern times.

John Coffee "Jack" Hays was a man who never boasted and never backed down, but he almost lost the gamble when he ambushed some 600 Indians with a company of forty Texas Rangers.

Indian Fighter

"Me and Red Wing not afraid to go to hell together. Captain Jack heap brave; not afraid to go to hell by himself."

While expressed by Flacco, a Lipan Indian scout, this opinion of John Coffee "Jack" Hays would not have been disputed by any man who ever rode with him.

A dark-haired, dark-eyed, soft-spoken, and apparently nerveless young man, Hays joined the Texas Rangers in 1839. During the next nine years he put a lasting imprint on this organization — setting the pattern, so to speak. He was a captain at twenty-three, a major at twenty-five, and a colonel at thirty-one — a rank he held in 1849 when he quit Texas for the California gold rush.

During his ranger service, Hays racked up a reputation for leadership and guts. He was a man who never boasted and never backed down.

Flacco's remark, however, came after Hays nearly got them both killed by accident. This happened during a fight when Hays's horse bolted through the middle of the Indian warriors, and Flacco, thinking his commander was making a charge, followed him. They both came out on the other side of the surprised hostiles unscratched, and circled back to join the rest of their company.

One of his contemporaries, J. W. Wilbarger, recalled Hays as "fitted by nature" for frontier service, being small, wiry "with such an iron constitution that he was enabled to undergo hardships and exposure without perceptible effect . . . I have frequently seen him setting by his camp fire at night in some exposed locality, when the rain was falling in torrents, or a cold norther with sleet or snow whistling about his ears, apparently . . . unconscious of all discomfort . . . often having eaten nothing more than a few nuts or hard-tack."

Born January 28, 1817, at Little Cedar Lick, Tennessee, Hays arrived in Texas shortly after the Battle of San Jacinto as a fully qualified surveyor. Later, this profession helped make him rich in California. But in Texas his main talent was as a fighter, both against Indians and Mexicans. His rank of colonel was held during the Mexican War.

The exploits of Hays earned him hatred and fear from the enemy and absolute loyalty from his men. His main "ace in the hole," however, was his recognition and use of the Colt revolver. He was first to use the weapon. After the federal government had turned it down as impractical, Hays insisted on it for his men. This gun gave him the edge even when vastly outnumbered.

Even so, he pulled some pretty fantastic "stunts" (as old-timers would describe his actions) — none more so than his last Indian fight on Texas soil.

During early 1846, as the Mexican War was about to get under way, Hays went chasing after some 600 raiding Comanche warriors. He managed to get ahead of them and set up an ambush. This with only forty young rangers at his back!

One of the rangers, E. M. Harrison, who later told about this experience, even used the term "fool-hardy" in describing the incident. To the rangers, anything Hays did seemed reasonable. (The official records of this fight burned in the state capitol fire of 1881.)

About nine months before the fight, Hays had been promoted to major and placed in command of the frontier battalion composed of Capt. R. A. Gillespie's and Capt. Ben McCulloch's companies. The former company was the only one Hays called upon to back him in this campaign. The two senior officers, Hays and Gillespie, represented the bulk of the experience for the group. Although Hays was known for "charging hell with a bucket of water," this fight at Paint or Painted Rock in Concho country was understandably later referred to as "one of the most desperate engagements with Indians on the Texas frontier."

Hays had come close this time to losing his gamble.

The rangers did cut the Indians off. Hays, having made an educated guess at where they were headed, beat them there. This was a small lake at the base of Paint Rock, where the rangers arrived at 1:00 A.M. following an almost nonstop ride of 130 miles in 42 hours.

"Major Hays placed his camp guards and allowed men and horses a needed rest," recalled Harrison. The rest was short, "for about daylight pickets reported Indians approaching and rangers made preparations to meet them."

The Indians, under the illusion they were safely in home territory, approached the lake in relaxed disorder. The rangers met them with a volley of fire, taking the vanguard by complete surprise.

As soon as it was full light, the Indians investigated the tracks of the rangers' horses and thought they knew the score — forty men. They fully expected to handle the situation in one assault.

For trooper Harrison, and probably most of the other young rangers, the start of the two-and-a-half-day battle left a lifelong impression: "I was a boy then, only 16 years old and tried to act as bravely as the more experienced rangers, but when I saw the long line of painted savages coming towards me in their first charge I felt the hair rise on my head and it seemed to me that all the devils from the lower regions had been turned loose upon us, but I braced myself and the panicky feeling passed away."

The rangers were between the Indians and the water, with their back protected by the outcropping of Paint Rock which rose 100 feet above the water. The lake measured about 100 yards wide and 300 yards long. The closest water to it was some twenty miles away.

Hays's only order to the men as the screaming Indians rode toward them was to "take good aim."

In the first onslaught a number of Indians were shot off their horses, but from then on they rode parallel to the rangers' position, shielding their bodies by hanging down on the offside of their mounts and shooting over their necks. While not considered anything more than a nuisance to the rangers trying to get them in their sights, such riding techniques had helped earn the Comanches their reputation for being among the world's best horsemen. Still, the Indians continued to lose men.

The attacks kept up all day. "The Comanches retired into the darkness, leaving their dead on the field," said Harrison, "but they continued to alarm the rangers' camp that night by small parties on foot, who were sent out for that purpose."

The Indians didn't attempt to reach the water, and according to Harrison, "it was necessary for them to ride twenty miles to the nearest water, but they left in small bodies and returned before morning. With these exceptions the night was uneventful."

The rangers rested during the night with Hays and Gillespie taking the watches, "though the usual detail had been stationed to guard the camp."

The second day of battle was much like the first. The rangers "repulsed charge after charge, and several followed in such succession that the men scarcely had time to reload their weapons."

By this time, says Harrison, the Indians knew the rangers were being led by their hated enemy "Captain Yack" (their name for him) "because he had made himself conspicuous at every vulnerable point throughout the fight."

This knowledge put more daring into the Indian charges: "the spirits of several hundred Comanche warriors who had been sent to the happy hunting grounds through his instrumentality was inciting them to vengeance," Harrison speculated.

When Harrison recalled the fight many years later, he said, "The rangers were in an extremely perilous situation that [second] night, and Major Hays realized the dangers that confronted him and especially the possibility of being attacked by the whole strength of the Comanche tribe, numbering several thousand warriors. It seemed as if he had invited destruction by penetrating so far beyond the nearest settlement with his small party of fearless men and cutting off a vastly superior body of Indians in the vicinity of their strongholds."

The rangers themselves were too tired and inexperienced to evaluate the situation themselves, undoubtedly trusting to Hays to get them out alive one way or another.

"Their endurance had been tested to the utmost, but all of them were young men whose energies would be restored by a few hours' rest and he let them sleep while he and Gillespie again assisted the outposts in guarding the camp or in repulsing small parties of the enemy who made occasional assaults," reported Harrison.

Climax to the battle came on the morning of the third day. The rangers, worn out and nearly out of ammunition, were awaiting a major onslaught around midmorning.

A very touchy situation, but Hays's phenomenal luck, ability, and marksmanship won out at almost the moment of disaster.

The Comanches "were led by a war chief who had been urging on the fight, and he exhibited a reckless bravery through the battle. He wore on his head the horns of a buffalo, with its heavy tuft of hair in front that covered his face . . . His body was clothed in a long buckskin garment with a heavy fringe along its edges and seams that had many paintings upon it which extended below the hips.

"He carried a long shield that protected his entire body, which was covered with a tanned buffalo hide so thick that a rifle bullet could not penetrate it."

However, when things were looking very grim for the rangers about midmorning, the war chief made a fatal mistake: "he [the chief] concentrated his entire force in one body and was leading the charge that probably would have overwhelmed the rangers . . . when the chief half turned to look back while urging his warriors forward, exposing his side. Major Hays instantly took advantage of his carelessness and sent a ball crossways through his body that killed him."

Loss of their leader proved to be too much for the warriors. After one last unsuccessful effort to retrieve the body of their chief, the Indians disappeared, apparently so upset at their loss they failed to notify four Indians left to guard the captured horses. These four were very shortly disposed of by the rangers.

Both Hays and Gillespie would have been in no doubt as to just how close the rangers had come to being wiped out — saved by no more than a moment's error by the Indian war chief.

In two and a half days of fighting, only one ranger had been wounded and one horse killed. All of which went to show, Harrison pointed out, that the Indians "could not compete with white men with improved arms under an intelligent leader."

Be that as it may, Hays couldn't wait to get the hell out of there, "though he would have preferred to remain and graze his horses that had been three days without food. He knew that his men were not in condition to pass through a similar experience, as they might have to do if he waited until the next day."

He also knew he had used up about all the luck he was going to get.

After reaching home camp, Harrison says, "The men and horses were completely fagged out . . . the expedition was exceedingly trying, especially on those not hardened in the service."

Even for Hays, it must have been a bit "trying."

In 1840 thirteen Comanche chiefs were cut down by Texans at the Council House in San Antonio when negotiations for the exchange of Indian captives broke down. The killings proved to be a major blunder by the Republic of Texas.

A Bloody Mess

Described as the greatest blunder in the history of Texas Indian relations, the Council House Fight of March 19, 1840, in San Antonio certainly hit an all-time low in diplomacy.

It was a bloody mess.

Four years after the fall of the Alamo, thirteen Comanche chiefs were slaughtered as they tried to fight their way out of a council being held in the courthouse in San Antonio. They were invited guests of the Republic of Texas.

On this occasion, some sixty-five Indians including the chiefs, their wives and children, were in town under presumably "a flag of truce" (whether it actually existed or not). The chiefs were there to discuss the return of white captives held by various Comanche bands.

The Texans thought the Indians would bring along the captives, but they brought only one. Either the Indians had not understood about bringing all the captives or chose to ignore this request. The young captive herself said the Indians deliberately didn't bring them, but planned to produce them one at a time for a higher ransom.

She would have done well to have kept her mouth shut. As it was, the Texas negotiators informed the chiefs they would be held as hostages until the captives were brought in. Upon hearing that pronouncement, one young chief drew a knife and headed for the door. When the smoke cleared, all thirteen chiefs were dead.

Chaos also broke out in the streets when the shooting started indoors, ending up with thirty-five Indians killed (not all of them male) and eight wounded. Seven Texans were killed and eight wounded. Some twenty-seven Indian women and children and two old men were captured.

To say the council had been a fiasco would be too mild a statement. Following what they felt was a betrayal, the entire Comanche nation went on the war path, after killing by torture most of the captives they had failed to bring in. Needless to say, the behavior of the Texans in San Antonio destroyed all future efforts to pow-wow with the Comanches.

For a couple of weeks after the fight, San Antonio was the scene of a number of dramas almost similar to aftershocks of an earthquake. But none of them had to do with any feelings of guilt — as far as either the military or civilians were concerned, the fight had been solely the fault of the Comanches.

Not long after the fight, a "brave and dashing" Comanche chief arrived to do mortal combat with the military commander. While this didn't take place, it led to a double killing by two dueling officers. In addition, the scientific interest of the local doctor in collecting "native bones" caused a furor, and to top everything off, a woman captive managed to escape and arrived in San Antonio.

All of these spinoff dramas were recorded by one of the town's leading ladies of fashion, a gently raised Southern belle, Mary Adams Maverick, whose matter-of-fact memoirs of this period are enough to make anyone a bit queasy.

A fairly recent arrival in San Antonio, Mary even mentions with seeming pride the marksmanship of her brother in shooting fleeing Indians on March 19. However, she was appreciative of the gallant bravery displayed by a defiant young Comanche chief who arrived on the scene in full war paint about a week after the council fight, obviously incensed over the recent murder of fellow tribesmen, if not actual family members.

As described by Mary, "Chief Isimanicaand along with another warrior rode boldly into the public square and circled around the plaza, then rode some distance down Commerce street and back, shouting all the while, offering to fight and heaping abuse and insults on the Americans.

"He was told through an interpreter that the soldiers were all down at the Mission San Jose de Aguayo. So, off they went to the mission, where the commander was sick in bed and Capt. Redd, the next in rank, was in command."

Mary reports that, much to the disgust of many, the captain told the chief: "We have made a twelve days' truce with your people, in order to exchange prisoners."

Others, of course, felt this arrangement had fallen through on March 19, but at any rate, the captain told the chief, "My country's honor is pledged, as well as my own, to keep the truce, and I will not break it. Remain here three days, or return in three days and the truce will be over. We burn to fight you."

The chief called him a liar and coward, along with other choice words, and then left with his friend, gathering up some 300 warriors waiting for him just out of town. He didn't come back.

This didn't end the matter. The chief wasn't the only one who thought the captain had behaved like a coward in not taking up the challenge. Capt. Lysander Wells, in town rather than at the mission at the time, received news of Redd's reply and wrote him a letter. This message not only spelled out his cowardice, but threw in his wife for good measure. If Wells was looking for a fight, he got one. Both participants in the resulting duel died.

Hopefully, the chief heard about it.

Another riot was nearly caused in town by the local doctor, Dr. Weidemann, described as a "cultured Russian scholar and naturalist." He had viewed the massacre as an opportunity to collect specimens of native skeletons. In order to render them down to the bones, "He stewed the bodies in a soap boiler, and when the flesh was completely desiccated, emptied the cauldron into the acequia," the ditch containing the town's drinking water.

Since most Texans, both Mexican and American, did not view Indians as people, the doctor's treatment of the dead did not upset the citizens. But tossing the remains into the drinking water did. There was even a city ordinance including a heavy fine forbidding the pollution of this water. When the doctor's methods for disposing of excess Indian leaked out, says Mary, "The people very properly, gathered in indignation, a mob rushed to the Mayor's office, the men talked in loud and excited voices, the women shrieked and cried . . . Many thought they were poisoned and would die."

The doctor was arrested and stood trial among a good deal of abuse from spectators who called him, *"diablo," "demonio,"* and other names. Mary reported, "He took it calmly, assured them the Indians had all sailed by in the night, paid his fine and went away laughing."

Apparently, the incident didn't affect his medical practice.

Then, on March 29, while San Antonio was still in a state of excitement, Mrs. Webster, the only adult survivor of the Webster wagon train massacre on Brushy Creek in 1839 (in which thirteen men were killed) staggered into town, carrying her four-year-old daughter Martha on her shoulders.

"The poor, miserable being was so unlike a white women that the Mexican hailed her as *Indio! Indio!* . . . She called out in good English however, saying she had escaped from Indian captivity."

Later, relating her twelve-day flight, Mrs. Webster said she had taken advantage of the departure of most of the braves when they left to attend the council meeting. She managed to escape with her daughter. (Her son, also captured in the attack, was with another band.) As the chief of the band holding Mrs. Webster was undoubtedly among the fatalities in the council chamber, her escape was just in time. There would have been little chance of her survival.

While at least thirteen captives were known to have died horrible deaths following the San Antonio debacle, a very few others were spared to exchange for the Indians captured by the Texans. During the following year, however, the Comanches and their allies more than evened the score by going on a rampage clear to the Gulf of Mexico.

The Council House Fight might at least have served the Texans as a good lesson in how not to treat or treat-with Indians. Unfortunately, it took history to point up the error of their ways. The Texans of 1840 didn't even notice.

For Texans, the Mexican War of 1846 was another great opportunity to even old scores. They fought courageously, losing many of their own, but their single-minded ferocious behavior terrified the Mexicans and horrified other American soldiers.

Sweet Revenge

"On the day of battle, I'm glad to have Texas soldiers with me, for they are brave and gallant, but I never want to see them before or afterwards, for they are too hard to control," wrote Gen. Zachary Taylor during the Mexican War of 1846–47.

Fact is, Texans were raring to go in this war. They had a lot of scores to settle with their old enemies south of the Rio Grande. Angry memories still festered over the martyrs of the Alamo and slaughter of Texas prisoners at Goliad, as well as the more recent systematic killing of Nicholas M. Dawson's men. Then there was the mistreatment of captured Texans who participated in both the Santa Fe and Mier expeditions during the days of the Republic.

Texans had more than enough grievances to go after the Mexicans. Unfortunately, they were far from selective in picking their targets — any Mexican would do.

Hostilities between Mexico and the United States began with little delay following American annexation of Texas. Mexico had never officially recognized Texas as being anything but part of its own territory and had warned the Americans to keep hands off.

However, Texans welcomed the fight. They threw themselves into the fray with all the enthusiasm of a personal vendetta. While never completely blending in with American troops, considering themselves more as allies, Texans furnished the highest proportion of troops to total population than any other state. This amounted to 8,018 volunteers and 222 regulars, totaling 8,240 — more men than it had taken Texas to win independence from Mexico in 1836.

Unfortunately, in their zeal to even the score the Texans managed to all but wipe from the record their real contribution to the final victory.

"All the Texas troops are anxious to go forward; they are hardy and can subsist on little," Taylor wrote, apparently finding it next to impossible to pay them any higher tribute. Praising Texans came hard to most regular American army officers, who simply were appalled at the "no-holds-barred," Texas style of fighting.

Commanding Texas forces at the Battle of Monterrey was J. Pinckney Henderson, who really had no business being there. He was governor of the newly designated State of Texas — a state whose constitution specifically forbids a military man from being head of state (just one of many instances when Texans made their own rules as they went along).

At any rate, in the Battle of Monterrey, Texans "exhibited unbounded courage" and had their first sweet taste of victory on Mexican soil.

The war was waged under two American generals: Taylor, who started the show off from the southern tip of Texas, and Winfield Scott, who replaced Taylor in command. (President Polk stripped Taylor of his command for moving against orders, directing him to return with his company to Matamoros.)

These politically inspired command changes didn't bother the Texans a bit. They had come to fight. Most of them had combat experience gained in the harsh realities of frontier fighting, where neither Indian nor Texan had ever heard of any rules of war. Some of those commanding the Texans were former rangers such as John C. "Jack" Hays, Ben McCulloch, Samuel H. Walker, and John S. "Rip" Ford, as well as Col. A. S. Johnson, commanding the First Texas Volunteers.

It was during this war that Rip Ford, already a legend, got his nickname. Texas casualties were heavy and in writing letters notifying families of a loss, Ford shortened the ending of "Rest in Peace" to just RIP.

Threat to the Republic of Texas of an impending Mexican invasion had been one strong reason most Texans welcomed annexation to the United States. Then, too, the majority of them came from the States and felt close ties anyway. Perhaps most important, Texans also recognized that without the help of the United States, chances of whipping the Mexicans a second time were all but nil. (Mexican President Santa Anna had underestimated the Texans on the first go-'round and wouldn't do it again.)

But, as far as this war was concerned, it was a very personal matter to the Texans whose attitude might be described as a tolerance for the U.S. Army — sort of "Glad to have you around, but stand back." Texans had their own ax to grind in this affair, and they were not about to let any military regulations get in their way.

As scouts and guerrilla fighters keeping supply lines and marching routes open, Texans performed invaluable service during the war. Their methods of clearing the enemy out of the line of march, whether blocked by soldiers or civilians, involved no gentlemanly rules of fair play — simply direct, deadly and final. Such behavior, while effective, overshadowed their gallantry, pure guts, and recognized value to the cause.

The Mexicans came to view the Texans with a mixture of pure hatred and terror. The officers and men of the regular United States Army viewed the Texans as they would a pack of wild dogs that happened to be helping them out at the moment. The Texans, spending most of their time in the saddle, looked the part. Although many were professional men — lawyers, doctors, merchants, surveyors — first and foremost they were Texans!

McCulloch's company, with the highest number of professional men, on one scouting mission rode 210 miles without taking off their boots. They were looking for the Mexican officer who had caused Santa Anna to have Ranger Ewen Cameron shot during the Mier death lottery of 1843, despite the fact that Cameron had drawn a white bean rather than the deadly black bean.

This side trip, of course, was unauthorized and they didn't find their man, but any Mexican *hombre* that got in their path was shot or hung.

Another Texas scouting unit under Maj. Walter P. Lane, heading more or less toward San Luis Potosi, took a small detour to the *hacienda* of Salado, where, in 1843, the black bean drawing had been held among the Mier prisoners. The bones of the executed Texans were collected and sent back to Texas under escort. They were later buried at LaGrange beside the Dawson casualties, where several Mier victims had relatives.

What upset regular career officers most about the Texans was that the Texans often returned from scouting expeditions with loot, but never with prisoners. There was one exception to this, when Hays arrived with a few prisoners in Mexico City, and Scott described the event as "one of the seven wonders of the world."

In command of the occupying Texas forces at the Mexican capital, Hays had already earned a reputation as an Indian fighter with very deadly views of the enemy. Shortly after arriving with the unexpected prisoners, some of his Texas troops got into a fight with a number of Mexican civilians who ended up killing a Texas ranger. Although Hays was not with this group, he refused to discipline them when the Texans returned to the run-down neighborhood and avenged their dead comrade by killing ninety or more Mexicans. Hays simply pointed out to "Old Fuss and Feathers" (as the Texans called

General Scott) that his men had to look after themselves. The general dropped the matter.

This incident certainly ended any habit the natives may have been developing to take pot-shots at Texans.

Later, when Santa Anna himself had to go through the Texas lines on a safe conduct pass issued by General Scott, the man who had given no quarter at the Alamo is said to have been extremely nervous, as well he might have been. All that kept the Texans from finishing Santa Anna off, pass or no pass, was Hays telling them that to do so would bring dishonor to Texas.

Even though Texans made it a point to give better than they received, they often came out pretty well battered.

This was the case at the Battle of Buena Vista. Captain Conner's company of fifty-seven men lost twenty-one dead or missing and two wounded. The only other Texans participating in this battle near the mouth of the Rio Grande were Major McCulloch and his twenty picked men, arriving when, wrote Taylor, "his own valuable services as a partisan and spy were greatly needed."

Later, Texans under Lt. Col. Samuel H. Walker took a mauling which included among the fatalities the commander himself. A former Mier prisoner, Walker had achieved the satisfaction of returning and retrieving a coin he had buried in the Prison of Peote outside Mexico City. His men are said to have cried when the tall redhead fell, mortally wounded. A Texas Ranger company, arriving on the scene right after the battle, mopped up the nearby town of Huamantla in retaliation.

However, after the American victory and occupation of Mexico City, Old Fuss and Feathers got fed to the teeth with Texans — even though the natives remained very passive wherever the Texas *"diablos"* went. The general finally managed to send them home.

During the next few years after the war, the federal government created a string of forts in Texas from the Rio

Grande to the Red River as a buffer against the hostile Indians. Almost all of them were named for fallen heroes of the Mexican War. Not one was named for a Texan.

If the Texans noticed the oversight, they didn't complain. The Mexican War had been nothing but satisfying to most Texans. What they wanted, they got . . . revenge!

The silver alarm watch went off at 3:30, frightening and amazing the Indians who believed it to be supernatural. Since Nelson Lee could make the watch "talk," it became his passport to life.

Captive Luck

It took a lot of guts, determination, and self-interest to survive in nineteenth-century Texas. And even then, without luck, it didn't always work out.

For a former Texas Ranger, Nelson Lee, luck tilted the scale in his favor. But for the others on the ill-fated California cattle drive of 1855, only those who got killed outright in the Indian attack were "lucky."

Lee's luck was in having bought a $45 alarm watch (a lot of money for that day) prior to starting the drive.

He later wrote that while in New Orleans he "discovered accidentally one day a large silver watch, of such unusual and extraordinary dimensions as to attract attention... So powerful was its internal machinery it would move across a common table whilst ringing the alarm."

Later, as the men proceeded from the mouth of the Rio Grande River, "following the grass" toward El Paso del Norte (El Paso), the large silver watch was part of Lee's gear.

Owners of the herd (Lee among them) had invested $7,000 in the venture, gambling on a rich return on their money when they reached the gold fields of California where meat was scarce. The hired hands on the drive were each to receive a horse, saddle, and $50 cash.

They all lost. Trail's end came during the early morning hours of April 2, in a beautiful grassy valley, perhaps in the Davis Mountains.

On this fatal cold and foggy night, Lee retired at midnight after standing first watch and setting his alarm for 3:30 A.M., the usual wake-up time.

Just short of this early morning hour, shrieking Comanches descended on the camp, killing and butchering all but four: Lee, one of his partners, William Aikens, and two other men. The captives were deliberately spared for further entertainment — torture, that is.

At the time, Lee recalled, "whether I was to be reserved for such a purpose or destined to be slaughtered on the spot, was a matter of terrible conjecture. With as much composure as was possible, in such trying circumstances, I awaited anxiously the issue."

For him, this was settled when one of the captors found his watch, which went off in the Indian's hand.

"Holding it out at extreme arm's length, his head thrown back, and staring wildly, the [Indian] was too much surprised, as it roared and rattled for two minutes, to decide whether it was safest to let it fall to the ground or retain it in his grasp."

As the Indians untied Lee's hands for him to make the watch "talk" again, the captive recognized an opportunity. Accepting the watch "with an air of reverence and adoration," he wound it up solemnly, and set it to go off again.

The ruse worked. The Indians thought he had a direct line to the Great Spirit — a point in his favor, but barely.

All four captives were paraded through the camp to view the butchered remains of their late companions, with the Indians indicating very clearly that their turn would come.

During the tour, the captives could also see why the "night watch" had failed them. The sentries had apparently been huddled together for warmth and "dispatched so suddenly there was no opportunity to make an outcry."

Then, in extreme discomfort, the captives traveled for several days to the main camp, where Lee and his alarm watch were presented to the chief. And Lee again went through a ritual to make it "talk."

However, his early fears of why the captives had been kept alive were soon confirmed. All four were bound to poles, the other two a short distance from Aikens and himself. And for four hours he and Aikens were forced to watch the slow torture-death of their companions, expecting that they themselves would be next in line.

Describing in his book *Three Years Among the Comanches* the torture and reaction of the two victims, Lee said, "I hung down my head and closed my eyes to shut out from sight the heart-sickening scene before me, but this poor comfort was not vouchsafed me. They would grasp me, as well as Aikens, by the hair, drawing our heads back violently, compelling us, however unwillingly, to stare directly at the agonized and writhing sufferers."

After the two finally were dispatched, says Lee, "Aikens and myself now anticipated we would be compelled to suffer the same fate, and endeavored to prepare ourselves to meet it."

The two, however, were cut loose from the poles and led away.

Following the experience of seeing his friends die such horrible deaths, as well as feeling it was only a matter of time before the novelty of the watch wore off or it broke, Lee refused to set the alarm. By other means, too, he tried to make his captors mad enough to kill him outright.

"If, therefore," he wrote, "I had previously feigned the character of a humble and devout missionary with some degree of success, I now played the part of an obstinate jackass to absolute perfection."

Fortunately, however, prior to Aikens being moved to another camp, where he expected to be (and probably was) tortured to death, the two were allowed to talk together. Aikens advised Lee to start cooperating and possibly save himself.

Lee took his partner's advice.

For three years, during which he and the watch were sold twice to other chiefs, he waited his chance to escape. His first attempt nearly resulted in his being permanently lamed when the chief cut the tendon below his knee on one leg.

"The muscle was not entirely severed, as was evidently his intention. The object of this surgical operation was to cripple me in such manner as to render escape impossible, even should a favorable opportunity present itself."

Before being traded off for the third and last time, Lee witnessed two more captive torture deaths — one an elderly white woman who could no longer work. Lee was incensed that the government couldn't give its citizens on the frontier the same protection rendered those in more populated areas or foreign countries.

During his captivity, he married a Comanche as another safeguard to his life, choosing the cleanest of several brides offered him.

Then in 1857 or '58, the moment he had been waiting for arrived.

Traveling alone with the chief, en route to a general Comanche war council, they stopped off for a night of drinking and carousing at another village. The next morning they set out again, Lee on a mule and the chief riding a fine horse, a knife thrust through his belt, a hatchet suspended from the pommel of his saddle, and a Mexican rifle, rare among his tribe.

Nursing a hangover and a mighty thirst, the chief got careless. Water was scarce and when they finally came to a small trickle from a seep, Lee could not fill the horn fast enough and the chief threw himself off the horse and down beside the stream.

It was his last mistake.

Lee left the chief's body beside the trickle of water and departed on the horse with all the weapons. The mule followed behind him.

For about two months Lee managed to survive in the arid mountains of what must have been the Big Bend country of West Texas. Twice he barely avoided encounters with Indians, he killed the mule for food, and finally had to abandon the dying horse.

"Very often while reclining on the ground, my feet resting on some little elevation to relieve pain, it seemed certain that sufficient energy would not return to permit me to rise again, and still more often I prayed God that when I fell asleep I might never wake again." Finally, "on the 58th day of my distressing travels," he was rescued by three Mexican traders en route home from a business trip among the Indians.

Lee ended his book with a plea that the government should do all it could to rescue the many white women being held among the various Indian tribes and bands. He suggested it would be easy to do this by using the traders to make the deals.

The watch had saved Lee initially, but he never could have survived the entire experience without being a really tough man to kill.

Hangings, arson, robberies, and other atrocities were heaped upon the man and his family who had voted to stay in the Union. At no time in Texas history have so many citizens, both civilian and military, shown such cruelty toward their neighbors and fellow Texans as during the Civil War.

Home Front Atrocities

Harassing, robbing, terrorizing, and murdering anyone known or suspected of Union sympathies became a gruesome sport throughout Texas during the Civil War. The extent of this downright meanness between Texans has been overlooked by most historians, relegated to a footnote, one might say, and understandably so. For one thing, the whole topic was rather taboo after the war. The survivors simply wanted to get on with their lives.

Although the majority of Texans did vote to secede from the Union in 1861, many were opposed. Joining the Confederacy was far from a unanimous choice. In many counties, particularly the German and western settlements and the northern border counties, sentiments were very pro-Union.

Little good it did them. The vindictiveness of the Confederate advocates has never been surpassed.

Those who stood up for staying in the Union paid dearly for their convictions. Some, of course, kept quiet and even fought for the Confederacy to avoid trouble. But many others felt they had a right to their own opinions and died feeling the same way about it.

Vigilantes, home guards, neighbors (sometimes so-called

preachers) preyed upon the defenseless to gain their property or sometimes just to "show 'em." But seldom was the issue based on any deep-seated political beliefs, other than perhaps just getting the opportunity to square off against anyone with the nerve to disagree with the majority. Those who might well have put a stop to the attacks were off fighting for the Confederacy, and when the war was over, they had problems of their own.

But no Unionist supporter — not even the Texas patriot and leader Sam Houston — was exempt from direct or indirect attack from those who advocated secession.

Houston, of course, paid with his political career. He was stoned, threatened, and verbally abused in every way when campaigning to keep Texas in the Union. And, even though one of his sons fought for the Confederacy, Houston — hero of the Texas Revolution, first elected president of the Republic and later governor and U.S. senator — was never again during his lifetime accorded any honors. While many of those who died would have counted Houston lucky to come out with a whole skin, he doubtless didn't feel that way.

The total number of Unionists who lost their lives or were forced to flee the state will never be known. As one writer noted, "Almost every county in this state had its hangings and murders of men who did not espouse the cause that was lost." Many were killed whether or not they attempted later to support the Union cause after the war actually started.

Take John R. Scott, for instance. Couldn't have been a finer man in Burnet County. A native of New York, and reared in New Jersey, Scott was, one might say, a born Unionist. Coming to Texas in 1851, he was a well-to-do respected man, living on Oatmeal Creek when the war broke out. He had served as the first county judge and made other contributions to the area.

None of these achievements saved him, nor the fact that four of his sons served in the Confederate army while he himself provided supplies to the Confederacy.

In this case, as in many others, the line between politics and greed was very blurred. Scott was considered a rich man. Looking back, one cannot help but wonder about the anonymous threats on his life and the friends who urged him to flee to Mexico and stay until after the war. One would hope there was no connection between the two factors, but, at any rate, he did take off for the border with $2,000 in gold strapped around his waist.

As the story goes, he stopped to spend the night with friends some seven miles from home. The next morning he was joined by a man named McMasters, also a Unionist.

Just before crossing a ford on the Colorado River between Smithwick and Marble Falls, they were held up. McMasters was robbed and hanged, Scott shot and robbed.

These details in themselves are curious, to put no finer point on the matter. Exactly where the deed was done would have been known only to the bushwhackers themselves; the bodies of their victims were disposed of several miles away from this crossing in what was known as Dead Man's Hole.

What was left of Scott, caught on a ledge in the deep hole, was not found until after the war. Scott's wife identified his remains by a peculiar jaw bone and teeth.

Several others of Burnet County labeled "Unionist" were likewise murdered, not the least of which was John R. Hubbard, a nephew of the Texas patriot Noah Smithwick — from which this community takes its name. Smithwick, veteran of the Texas Revolution, had earlier recognized there would be no coexistence between Confederate and Unionist and lit out for California. He had left his mill, near the present site of Smithwick, in the hands of his nephew.

According to Hubbard's biography in the Burnet County history, Hubbard was murdered just prior to departing for California. His body was thrown into a hole of water on Cow Creek in southeastern Burnet County. Today, a falls near that hole of water is known as Hubbard Falls.

Smithwick, referring to this and other murders of Unionists during the war (while making it clear he had no grudge against the Confederate soldier who fought the Yankees), wrote: "... but for the cowards who, taking good care to keep out of harm's way, hunted down and murdered defenseless Union Men — well, I have never been a believer in the orthodox hell; still, when I think of those wretches, I am forced to concede that it was an oversight in the plan of creation if hell was left out."

Smithwick wasn't the only one to express this thought. James Wilson Nichols, who was finally forced to leave Blanco County, wrote in his journal of innumerable atrocities committed against his fellow Unionists. These included the wanton killings of both young and old, hanging four at one time from a tree and refusing to let their wives cut them down for burial. Children who wouldn't tell or didn't know where their fathers could be found were beaten and often killed.

Nichols, a very religious man, summed up his feeling with: "I say, if they [the vigilantes] could through any means escape the punishment to which their crimes so justly entitle them, then I should lose faith in an omnipotent God and wonder for what purpose hell was instituted."

The title given Nichols's journal, *Now You Hear My Horn,* by the editor, Catherine W. McDowell, comes from his answer to threats on his own life: "... if they want to hang me they can find me right here at the end of two [dou]ble barel [shot guns]. We can git as many of you as you can of us and the first man that crosses that fence is my meat. Now you hear my horn."

The vigilantes gave Nichols a wide berth, but finally harassed him out of the county with trumped-up lawsuits.

But, while many local civilians showed a vicious, greedy side — unmatched even in the worse Indian raids — two of the most contemptible mass murders of Union sympathizers were committed by men wearing Confederate uniforms. In both of these separate incidents, the murdered men were simply taking advantage of a state decree giving Union sympathizers thirty days to leave Texas. They were openly and confidently headed for Mexico.

Of these, the most publicized was what came to be known as the Battle of the Nueces, August 2, 1862. Nearly fifty Unionists, primarily from German communities, were camped when attacked without warning during the early morning hours. The ill-armed Germans fought back, killing some ten men and wounding forty-five, while losing nineteen of their own during the battle. Nine others were so seriously wounded that they could not withdraw. These wounded were shot in cold blood.

Giving the orders to kill helpless men was James E. Duff, a former San Antonio shopkeeper who had organized his own ranger unit. He ordered all the bodies left on the field as "an example to other unionist[s]." Families and friends later gathered up and buried the bones in a mass grave at Comfort.

Prior to this infamous attack, Duff had already shown his stripe by instituting a reign of terror throughout the Hill Country — killing and robbing Union sympathizers.

But the incident which can't be topped for pure brutality occurred in 1863 when a much smaller group, eight men and a boy, from Williamson County headed for Mexico. With no thought of danger, they stopped to buy supplies in Bandera.

The group was "well provided with good mounts, heavily armed, possessed several hundred dollars in cash and were fully equipped for the long journey to the neutral republic on the other side of the Rio Grande," says the account in *One Hundred Years in Bandera 1853–1953*.

The author and publisher of this work, the late J. Marvin Hunter, while pointing out the "gratifying" fact that the perpetrators of the crime were not from the county, spares the reader none of the gruesome details. Confederate cavalrymen from Camp Verde, twelve miles north of Bandera, are given full credit.

The Confederates overtook the small band of Unionists and started back to Camp Verde with their prisoners, only to decide to hang them en route. A few of the Confederates would have nothing to do with the murder and rode off. Under the command of the Confederate major, seven of the men were hanged one at a time by strangulation, the eighth was shot with the ramrod left in the gun to spear him. The boy was taken off by the Confederates and "never heard of again."

Although the murderers were never arrested, they were charged, and says Hunter, "the court records of Bandera county will reveal the names of the men who stood charged with the crime of murdering helpless prisoners." This in itself was a great improvement over most of the other crimes against Unionists in which no one was ever charged.

Another mass killing came to be known as "the Great Hanging at Gainesville" in October 1862. This was somewhat wrapped up in legality by what in some quarters might have been a sincere fear of the Unionists taking over.

The discovery of an alleged "Peace Party Conspiracy" triggered the action by the Confederate army. Some 200 men were rounded up in several counties. But, after collecting the suspected conspirators, the military turned all but three (who were Confederate soliders) over to a "citizens' court." The fact that a "lynching tree" rather than a scaffold was used to hang nineteen condemned by the civilians, along with the three additional soldiers found guilty by the court-martial, puts the whole procedure into the same pot with other terrorist actions statewide.

The lot of a Unionist in Texas during the Civil War was heart-sickening.

Nichols perhaps said it best when he described the murderers and tormentors (in his own spelling) as a: "rotten harted, thieving, savage set of hypocritical, fraudalent purgered and poluted set, ring click, vecesh, kid glove, paper collar, brass stud, mooving mass of coruption."

Kids, mostly ranging in age from eight to sixteen, who joined the Home Guard during the Civil War earned the names of "Heel-Flies" by making life miserable for anyone they could bully.

Heel-Flies

Heel-flies, the pesky insects said to be the only living things capable of getting the better of a wild Longhorn, had their human equivalent in Texas during the latter part of the Civil War.

These were the kids, mostly under sixteen years of age, recruited into Home Guards. And, according to one who had experience with them, these boys represented "a stench to the nostrils of all decent men."

Overbearing, troublesome and mean, the Home Guards helped make life miserable not only for Union sympathizers, but anyone else they could bully.

"Such was the high-handed, outrageous conduct of the Home Guards, not only in a few sections but throughout the state generally, that they obtained the sobriquet of 'Heel-Flies' on account of the similarity of their course to the tortuous proclitivities of a pestiferous insect so well known to cattlemen all over Texas." So wrote John Warren Hunter in 1870, a man with the personal experience to back up his assessment of these youngsters.

Tantalizing reference to Heel-Fly outrages crops up from time to time in various stories of Civil War days in Texas, but one of the few, if not the only, writer to lay it on the line was Hunter, founder of *Hunter's Magazine* (forerunner of *Frontier Times*). Chances are the former guardsmen remained a dangerous bunch of young men to cross even after the war, when those who knew them best could have spoken up.

Hunter noted that after they were organized into a company, the Home Guards usually were moved out of the county where family members and other adults might have been able to restrain them. "These rawhide soldiers soon became a terror to the people among whom they were thrown," he said.

Paid in worthless Confederate money, poorly equipped, and given more authority than they knew how to handle, these young hellions managed to take up the slack by running roughshod over one and all, irrespective of sex, age, or physical condition.

During the latter part of the war, when casualties, illnesses and desertions had reduced the Confederate army to a dangerous level, a conscript law was enacted requiring all able-bodied men to report for duty.

The Home Guards were organized to help round up the reluctant, as well as to catch deserters. They also helped collect tithes on wool, grain, and cotton for the Confederacy, and otherwise made themselves useful. Most of the adult male population was off fighting or attempting to avoid the duty.

As it became obvious the Confederacy would fall, a great many Texas soldiers simply picked up their guns and headed home from the various battles where friends, relatives, and enemies lay sprawled on the field. When caught by the guard, or regular Confederate soldiers, they were court-martialed, shot, or sent off to hard labor in Galveston and Houston.

As a result, the woods, bogs, and river bottoms filled up with men of all types who hid out until the war was over.

The Home Guards, out from under parental guidance and often taking orders from a beardless youth, not only took to their duties with gusto but added a number of other "shakedowns."

Heel-Flies would stop a returning soldier furloughed for sickness or battle wounds. The veterans would be stopped "by these arrogant stripplings and anything worthwhile demanded of them. If they chanced to be well mounted and carried valuable arms, a flaw was found in their papers, these had to be sent to Houston or Austin for further scrutiny, while the unfortunate soldier who had passed through the carnage of battle at the front had to remain in the guard house until their papers came back" — unless willing to part with horse, weapons, and/or cash, in which case he was allowed to escape.

Sometimes, when the only thing of value was the soldier's six-shooter, he was relieved of this as a "forced loan." The owner was informed that while off-duty he had no use for a six-shooter; that the guard needed it since they were in active service for their country; and that when he got ready to start back to the army he could have his pistol. The gun was never seen again by its owner.

There were some exceptions, of course. A few young guardsmen on the frontier were kept busy fighting Indians and some others joined the guard to protect their families suspected or known for Unionist sympathies. But most were just young, wild kids.

At the time of his encounter with them, Hunter was not much older than the guardsmen themselves. This fact may have given him the added contempt to disregard any danger these young men might still have posed after the war.

Hunter had planned to join the Confederate army, but he changed his mind when an older friend was hanged along with a number of other Union sympathizers. Completely disillusioned, Hunter "resolved to never lift a musket against the old flag." So at age fifteen he went to wait the war out in Mexico.

While in Matamoros, across from the lower tip of Texas, he took a commission to reenter the state and secure a team of mules for another ex-patriot. Blue-eyed, blond, and fair-skinned, Hunter's disguise as a native Mexican, who spoke no

English, was viewed with suspicion by all Texans, especially the members of the Home Guard.

In the course of his trip, Hunter twice was arrested by these young men. Fortunately, none of them spoke Spanish as his own accent was far from that of a native. However, on the first occasion, the Spanish-speaking citizen, brought in to expose him, opted to back his story up. The second time he made a run for freedom.

A man's main defense against the Home Guard, says Hunter, was their inexperience, poor mounts, and lack of good weapons. The Heel-Flies were "armed with such weapons of destruction . . . as hunting or squirrel rifles of ancient pattern, single barrel shotguns, pepper-box pistols, an occasional Enfield and six-shooters." The latter were acquired by threat or outright robbery from either soldiers or civilians.

According to Hunter, the Heel-Flies had not only mean dispositions but iron constitutions to match their temperaments, being able to drink with apparent relish what Hunter described as "the most villainous decoction of liquid damnation I ever tasted." The spirits cost two-bits a drink, hard cash, and Hunter noted that "if there was ever a concoction that would make a rabbit spit in a bull dog's eye, slap his ears, and dare him to mortal combat, that Pine Top Whiskey was certainly the real article."

On his trip to get the mules, Hunter says, "I crossed the San Antonio river at Goliad. Here I encountered the Heel-Flies and here my troubles began. I had not proceeded half way across the public square when I was surrounded by about twenty boys and one or two old men, who informed me that I was under arrest and must give an account of myself."

Pretending not to speak English, Hunter says, "They took hold of my bridle and with drawn pistols led me to the commandant's office." This man turned out to be the "enrolling officer" or recruiter, "a dapper little bunch of hair and bluster."

Hunter said the captain told him "he could smell a greaser anywhere and I didn't look like a Mexican to him."

Fortunately, when the captain did locate someone who spoke Spanish fluently and could tell immediately that Hunter was no Mexican, it turned out to be the daughter of a Union sympathizer who was in prison. She vouched for Hunter being a native Mexican and he was set free.

His next encounter wasn't quite as easy. Hunter was preparing to return to Mexico, hiding his pistol in a morral that hung at his saddle bow, his lunch and some other items on top. When the Heel-Flies picked him up just outside Columbus, Hunter says, "At no time had I worn my pistol while in Columbus, as I knew the cupidity of these Heel-Flies and not having seen me armed at any time, I suppose accounts for the fact that when arrested they made no attempt to search me."

On this occasion, Hunter was given an hour to bring in Mexican witnesses to verify that he was indeed a native of Mexico. The Home Guard commander told Hunter, "You may be a Mexican but I don't believe it. And see that your witnesses tell the truth. You bring a lot of greasers in here to lie for you and I'll have every one of you shot."

Fortunately, the Heel-Flies were preoccupied with another prisoner as Hunter circled the block, came back around, and mounted his unguarded, saddled horse at the hitching rack in front of the Home Guard headquarters.

But it wasn't long before the Heel-Flies were in hot pursuit.

Outdistancing them on his better mount, Hunter says, he turned to look back: "A hasty glance showed a straggling string of horsemen — all enlisted in the chase. I waved my hat, gave a cheer and offered those nearest me a very profane remark in good clear plain English."

Although Hunter's experience with the guard was mostly concerned with their overbearing treatment of the populace, other references indicate they were not above murder, looting, and destroying the homes of Union sympathizers.

Later, after his salutation to his pursuers, Hunter thought again he was about to be caught by them. It turned out to be a false alarm, but he says, "I swore to myself if I managed to get out in one piece, I'd never be caught again in the Heel Fly range."

Before finally reaching Matamoros, Hunter met up with other Unionists, Heel-Flies, Confederate soldiers, and organized deserters. It was a trip he never forgot, but of the Heel-Flies he was most contemptuous: "No class of men or rather striplings, in our great state has ever been the recipient of more righteous contempt heaped upon them by patriotic men and women of Texas than these Home Guards."

As daylight dawned, the French brothers surprised their first victims, camped during a cow hunt, and shot them both before they were fully awake.

Vengeance

Even in an age when bloody vendettas were common-place — following the Civil War, that is — the French brothers made a real impression.

In 1865, when Jim and Dick French arrived home from service in the Frontier Rangers, they found their father had been arrested for murder and taken to San Antonio for trial. Rushing off after him, they arrived in the city too late. Their daddy had been hung from a chinaberry tree in the main plaza.

The deed had been done by members of a vigilance committee who had taken the senior French away from the arresting officers just as they arrived with him in San Antonio.

Unfortunately, for the vigilantes, the French brothers knew, or soon discovered, the names of all the members of the committee. They were people from their own "neighborhood" whom they had known all their lives.

Hatred wouldn't even begin to describe the brothers' feelings at this point.

The fact that their father might have deserved hanging, for the brutal murder of two Mexican cattle buyers, had little or nothing to do with the subsequent attitudes expressed by local citizens or the personal vendetta waged by the sons.

As far as the neighbors were concerned, the sons were expected to avenge their father, and the fact that they did not begin to do so immediately "showed a lack of grit."

But despite their youth (both were in their early twenties) the French brothers realized to take immediate action would defeat their purpose. "They would probably be hanged themselves before they could exact one half of the vengeance that would satisfy their wrath," says the teller of their tale, R. H. Williams, under whom the brothers had served in the frontier rangers during the Civil War. So they waited.

Williams describes the two affectionately as "dare-devil boys and first rate frontiersmen."

Williams certainly recounts the story of the French brothers' attempt to settle the score with their father's murderers in nothing but supportive terms.

An English soldier-of-fortune, Williams came to Texas in 1861, served in the Confederate army, and later was a Texas Ranger. He returned to England in 1868, and forty years later wrote about his experiences in *With the Border Ruffians*.

After the shock of discovering the lynching of their father, the French brothers, he says, returned to the family ranch, located near the Leona River southeast of Uvalde. There they proceeded to lay low.

Those who didn't buy the apparent nonchalance of the French brothers were the leaders of the lynching party — Hiram Minshull, his father Asa, and Sol Chiff. The uncharacteristic quiet apparently scared them half to death, and during what proved to be the lull before the storm, they cleared out, "probably to Mexico."

Other members of the committee stayed, viewing the passive appearance of the brothers with relief. Within six months, says Williams, if the hanging was recalled at all, it was only because the sons had taken it so quietly. Vigilante action was too common an occurrence to cause too much of a stir.

But, even with the departure of the leaders, the French brothers did not rush into action. There still remained plenty of the vigilantes to satisfy their cravings to get even.

When they did start, Williams appears to have been in complete accord with the brothers — not only in killing the actual members of the vigilante committee, but any friends or relatives who happened to be with them when the brothers arrived on the scene.

The deadly hunt got under way in May 1865, several months after their father had been lynched. It was a well-chosen time as the state was between Confederate and Union control — the first having dissolved in defeat, and federal occupation not yet completely in place. Whether the brothers were aware of this fact, or chose the time for fear all their quarry would further scatter, is unknown.

At any rate, they set out well-mounted and armed with a couple of six-shooters and a repeating rifle apiece. As daylight dawned, they surprised their first victim and his friend camped during a cow hunt, and shot them both before they were fully awake. The bodies were left on the ground while the brothers took off for their next target.

Here, at breakfast time, they expected to find the committee member (and his two sons with whom they had served in the rangers). Although former comrades-in-arms, the sons of the vigilante who had helped murder their father were now hated enemies. However, much to the French brothers' regret, only the father himself was at home. As he emerged from the cabin in the early morning light, he received a volley of shots.

"The young ruffians dragged the body into an outhouse close by and then sat down coolly to breakfast in their victim's house," says Williams.

Three men dead and the day just beginning.

However, it must have been the next day before they sighted another victim. "The news that the French boys were on the shoot had reached him," says Williams. He was, in fact, trying to put distance between himself and the avengers when he spotted the brothers bearing down on him.

Making a race for his home, the fleeing man turned in the saddle to shoot, but missed. "In desperation, he pulled his horse sharp around to get a fair aim but the poor animal was done and his rider came heavily to the ground . . . and before he could rise, [the French brothers] put two bullets into him where he lay, and so slew their fourth man."

Another vigilante, who had not gotten the word, had taken some cows to Mexico with his son. It took the French boys several days to intercept the father and son heading home. They were "nooning it under the shade of some live-oaks, hard by a water-hole."

The brothers greeted them, got off their horses, exchanged news, and waited until the two were saddling up before shooting. The son was killed outright, but the wounded father was hung to the tree limb under which they had just been chatting.

They were by this time about out of vigilantes. Their last known killing took place in a saloon in Atascosa, where the target was found having a drink with a friend. Both were killed. One of the brothers was wounded, but apparently not seriously.

"Then," says Williams, "as coolly as though nothing had happened they both walked out of the saloon, six shooters in hand, no one daring to hinder them."

Shortly after this encounter, Williams ran into his former subordinates, who filled him in on all the details of their activities. Apparently, they couldn't have had a more sympathetic listener.

The French brothers were last seen headed for Mexico to hunt down the leaders of the vigilante committee who had run for cover.

But, explains Williams, with what appears to be a note of regret, "As for their quest for Asa Minshull, it was most improbable they would succeed in it, for the old villain was far too cute to stay in Matamoros, even if he had gone there . . . Most likely he had gone up North straight away, and was by that time a shining light in some Methodist church in Boston, or elsewhere."

Even so, from Williams's story, the French brothers weren't much on giving up. The vigilantes would have done well to have let the law handle old man French.

Two outlaws, John Wesley Hardin and Bill Longley, met only once in a poker game but were well aware of each other's careers. Neither one was "over burdened" with honor.

Two of a Kind

Tough kids — cold-blooded killers who would shoot first and think later, if at all — were commonplace in Texas following the Civil War. Two of the worst were John Wesley Hardin and Bill Longley. Both got a real kick out of killing.

Wild Wes and Bad Bill, tags given them by later writers, started their outlaw careers while still in their early teens — Wes, fifteen, and Bill, sixteen or seventeen. Each killed a Negro and ran for cover. Wes followed this up by ambushing the four soldiers sent to capture him, gunning them all down.

While both later insisted that the carnage they created (Wes credited with forty-four murders, Bill thirty-two) all came about in self-defense, it just wasn't so.

These boys were plain mean.

As Longley once put it: "I do not feel as far as Wes Hardin is concerned in the matter of honor, that neither Hardin nor myself are over burdened."

What Wes thought of Bill is not known. The first and perhaps the only time they met was in a poker game. Longley had already established a reputation for being dangerous to cross and usually didn't allow any man to leave a game a winner until he himself was ready to quit.

On this occasion, Wes left the game about $300 ahead. Later, when asked why he had allowed this to happen, Longley reportedly replied: "This kid's got the eyes of a killer — cold and crazy! I don't mess with that kind unless the blue chips are down and it's me or them. Bad medicine!"

In a day when outlaws were a dime a dozen in Texas, these two stood out. But they had lots of company. For almost a decade, outlaws called the shots in Texas. Legal law held little threat to anyone with a fast horse. Danger came from other outlaws, reward hunters, and vigilantes.

With the military in occupation during Reconstruction, and all the state legislative and legal power in the hands of Yankees of one sort or another, former Confederates were forced to look out for themselves. Settling disputes, whether of a civil or criminal nature, was taken care of in the most direct way without the help of what was considered a rigged court. Quite often the man with the fastest draw won the case.

At first, the kids who had gotten out of hand during the war were viewed with tolerance by family, friends, and neighbors. Both Wes and Bill started out by killing Negroes who offended them for one reason or another. And, as long as the shootings involved former slaves, Yankees, Mexicans, or Indians, little notice was taken by most Texans.

This sympathetic attitude quickly wore off when the targets became general, involving anyone for just about any reason, or no reason at all.

In the 1870s, when Hardin and Longley were out of control, literally hundreds of killers roamed the state as individual bandits or members of outlaw gangs. No man was safe; all carried guns.

Getting away with murder during these years was considerably easier than surviving as a horse thief or rustler. Both those latter crimes were automatically hanging matters, while shooting a man down might or might not be of any consequence.

Longley had an early lesson in the danger of rustling

when he and a friend were caught branding the wrong cow. They were promptly hung to a nearby tree (slow strangulation for most victims). One of the vigilantes turned in his saddle as he rode off, letting go with a number of shots at the hanging men. One of these cut the rope holding Longley. He survived (his partner did not) and for Longley it ended any desire to make a living off another man's stock.

As for Hardin and Longley, there was little to choose between them. It was a fact well known to them both. Longley complained about the unfairness of it all when awaiting trial and expecting the worse. He pointed out in a letter to the court: "... don't you think it is rather hard to kill me for my sins and give Wes Hardin only twenty-five years for the crimes he has committed?"

In view of both their records, the injustice lay in not hanging Hardin. In fact, Longley had little to complain about. Some of his killings were quite messy and uncalled for — an elderly preacher, an unarmed friend, an unsuspecting stranger, to mention but a few.

Longley had an engaging manner and many friends, but he killed without compunction anyone who crossed him.

His last killing — the one that got him hanged — was a deliberate, cold-blooded shooting down of an unarmed man. One version (certainly not his own "fair fight" one) says as he rode up to the field where Wilson "Wilsie" Anderson was plowing, walking behind the mule and singing a hymn, Bill waited for him to make one more round, presumably to finish the song, then shot him down without warning.

Longley felt Wilsie was responsible for the death of his cousin, Cale Longley, while Wilsie had claimed Cale died from an accidental fall from his horse. Cale's family didn't buy this explanation, so Wilsie paid with his life. But, on the other hand, so did Bill.

Hardin also had strong family feelings. Clan loyalties ran deep in most Texas families. When his cousins, the Clements brothers, became embroiled with their Taylor kinsmen in the bloody Sutton-Taylor Feud in 1873–74, Hardin made it his own fight. It was expected of him.

Although one writer described Hardin as "the deadliest gun-fighter the West ever produced," he was pretty much a product of the time. He considered those who fell under his gun as deserving the end he provided; he expressed no regrets and offered no apologies.

Longley did regret one killing, that of a stranger who attached himself to Longley for their mutual protection in going through some dangerous country. Longley shot him while he slept. Some say it was because the man's snoring kept Longley awake, but Longley said the stranger appeared nervous and that worried him. It turned out that the man was, like Longley, on the dodge from the law.

An outlaw couldn't be too careful, of course. Many a man would have liked to pick up the reward for their capture.

Hardin finally killed the wrong man. Ironically enough, it was as near self-defense as Wes ever came. He was in Comanche, Texas, when a deputy sheriff attempted to arrest him. The deputy had made a fatal mistake, but in a way, so had Wes. When he managed to elude the mob, several other members of his family were hanged out of hand. The deputy was also a former and popular Texas Ranger, and this put the hounds on Hardin's heels until they finally ran him to ground in Florida.

The outlaw era came to an end shortly after Wes went to prison and Bill was hanged in Giddings (quipping as he stumbled on the steps of the rickety gallows October 11, 1878: "Look out there. Let's don't get crippled up before the show is over.").

Texas Rangers working from a list of over 400 known outlaws, along with various citizen groups (vigilantes), finally mopped up the mess — killing some and running most other rascals out of the state.

Hardin, following parole some years later, ended up being shot in the back as he sat throwing dice for drinks in an El Paso saloon. His often quoted last words, "Four sixes to beat

. . .," might have served as an epitaph except for the better one given by a local citizen of El Paso. Upon hearing the argument as to whether Hardin had died in a fair fight or foul, the El Pasoan replied, "Either way is okay far's I'm concerned, just so long as the bastard's dead."

That sort of sums it up for all of them.

Citizen committees or vigilantes wasted little time and no sympathy on suspected outlaws, who were later found shot or hanged. Committeemen, however, attempted to keep their own identities secret for legal and safety reasons, with varying amounts of success.

Vigilantes

When local citizens finally got fed up with outlaws running wild, "they fed them from the same spoon." Horse thieves, robbers, murderers, rustlers, and other undesirables found themselves up against a deadly foe — the vigilantes.

During the 1870s and '80s, secret vigilance committees operated in practically every county in Texas, ruthlessly stomping out outlaws like so many rattlesnakes.

As Parson Merony, a preacher at the Grove Community in Bell County, put it when asked about lynching outlaws, "Well, it's a business I wouldn't like to engage in, but thank God, there are men who will do it."

That was the general opinion: get rid of the outlaws by whatever means available.

It was a very bitter dosage. No quarter was asked and none given on either side. Often the suspected or known outlaw was taken to the nearest tree and left hanging by his neck as a warning to his friends.

Other times, the vigilantes chose to lay in ambush for their quarry, strung out along the road or trail where their victim was expected. If the first shot missed, one of the others down the line would finish the job off. Often, if not usually, the killings involved not one but two or more victims.

Some committees were highly organized with captains, secret passwords, whistle signals, and execution squads. Others were loosely held together, simply rising to the occasion when required.

Most committees were known only by their deeds. Understandably enough, the members did not want their names attached to the various downright murders that helped to bring a measure of peace and tranquility to various parts of the state. This has, of course, made for considerable misinformation and has relegated these secret societies to the shadows of Texas history.

Fortunately, in the case of the vigilantes who took care of the outlaws known as the Notch Cutters of Yegua Creek, there exists some excellent second-hand information. Sons of two of the vigilantes tried to clarify what actually happened in separate stories during the 1960s.

Both writers received the information from their respective fathers many years after the events, and were writing about them after even more years. Naturally, all of the details do not agree between the two accounts, but they are near enough to give a clear picture of very dangerous times.

The scene for both the Notch Cutters and the vigilantes who took after them included a wide circle where the three counties of Williamson, Lee, and Bastrop come together. The Notch Cutters had such a firm grip on the region that it took some eight years to break their hold, and two decades and more to end the "troubles."

With more confidence than sense, these outlaws gained their name by cutting notches on their gun stocks or gun handles for each kill. These markings became a dead giveaway after the vigilantes went into action in the mid-1870s.

Versions vary as to whether these vigilantes were organized into one large secret society involving men from all three counties, or consisted of separate interlocking committees woven together with couriers keeping each informed of major decisions.

At any rate, the sons of two of the vigilantes, Luckett P. Bishop, Sr., writing for the *Frontier Times* of June/July 1965, and G. K. Martin, whose story appears in the Spring 1969 issue of *Old West,* agree completely on the efficiency, relentlessness, and secrecy of the membership.

Bishop had been raised in the McDade area and Martin grew up in the Knobbs (Knobs) community — both centers for much of the bloody action. While neither one was old enough to witness the actual dramas involved, the repercussions were still being felt during both of their lifetimes.

Although outlaws were prevalent all over the state, in this particular area the difficult terrain, brush, and trees along Yegua Creek had made it an ideal hiding place for "dodgers" from the Confederate army, as well as other low types. In addition, many of the younger generation of the pioneer families in the area became attracted to the excitement of the outlaw's life.

For a number of years, the Notch Cutters had little to fear from the law-abiding citizens, who took the killing of strangers as none of their business. But, when the outlaws started robbing and killing the neighbors, the heat was on.

As the vigilantes moved in to put a lid on the situation, there was little room for sentiment. A well-respected man whose kid had gone bad was just as likely as not to find him hanging from the limb of a tree. Martin says this situation caused a lot of heartaches in the Yegua Creek area.

Most vigilance committees met secretly, considered a list of names of suspected outlaws to eliminate, and voted their decisions. In the case of the Yegua Creek vigilantes, a captain would then quietly designate the actual members who would do the job. Some members were never called upon to do the killings.

Sometimes, of course, action was taken without calling any meeting. Such individualists as the Olive brothers asked for no help. At least three of the brothers were undoubtedly members of a vigilante committee (probably to assure that the name of a wilder younger brother did not appear on any execution list). But the Olives posted their own warnings and took direct action with those who didn't heed them.

The Olive ranch, located in the southern part of Williamson County, not far from McDade, was well within the Notch Cutters' domain. Although some of their own cattle were suspect as to origin, the family became very possessive once the Olive brand was slapped on. Thus, when two men were caught skinning Olive cows, the thieves were wrapped up in the wet skins — the brand visible on the outside. Most sources say the victims were shot first, but a more gruesome version would have it that the men were left to die as the hides shrunk.

At any rate, this was not a "voted on" action of the vigilantes.

But, when men were taken from a saloon or a dance by masked men, there was no doubt in anyone's mind that the main body of vigilantes were in action.

Martin pointed out the vigilantes "tried not to involve innocent men, but in their wide sweep of activities, probably some who were guiltless were killed."

How well organized the Notch Cutters were is hard to tell. At any rate, they appear to have been well known to one another and acted as a pack of wolves, two or more being in on every kill.

In the beginning, the Notch Cutters preyed upon the traveler passing through the region. Prior to the shock of having well-respected neighbors gunned down and robbed, the locals took a detached interest. It was a matter of speculation as to who they might be when two well-dressed strangers were found hanging from the same tree limb, or another victim was left naked in a field. There was no mystery as to who was responsible.

All of this changed to rage when a respected farmer was

robbed and killed while en route home with his crop money. Vigilantes came into being, and the war was on.

Many versions of this conflict between the "good and the bad guys" in this three-county area have been written, in addition to that of the sons. Helen Rummell wrote a story which appeared in the July 1930 *Frontier Times,* reprinted from the *Austin American-Statesman.* She made up in dramatic action what her story lacked in accuracy. However, she did add some color to at least one well-documented event — a local dance near the Knobs which ended with four of the guests required to do a "dead man's jig" from limbs of a nearby tree.

On June 27, 1879, an area citizen, Pat Earhart (Irehart), famous for his parties, hosted one of the most memorable dances in the history of Lee County. Rummell described Earhart as the McDade singing master and dancing fiddler (others described him as a prosperous bachelor, a dapper dresser, a rather mysterious gentleman farmer). He may or may not have known in advance what was in store for several of his guests.

Five young men, said to be having their last fling before seeking safer territory, were targeted by the vigilantes to die that night.

About 2:00 A.M., when the dance was in full swing, every door and window bristled with gun barrels pointing into the room. The host was handed a list of names to read out. The vigilantes wore their hats low on their foreheads, and handkerchiefs covered their lower faces. None of them spoke a word — according, that is, to the best account.

All of the male guests had been relieved of their guns upon arrival — a strict rule of the house. Four of the five whose names were read out stepped forward. Vigilantes tied their hands behind their backs and nudged them out the door with their gun barrels. These men were Wade Alsup, Young Floyd, John Kuykendall, and Bake Scott; the fifth, Jim Floyd, was not in the room. One account speculates he was out back when the vigilantes rode up and "not having any curiosity about what they wanted, he left the country."

Those present to answer the roll call didn't last long. They were marched 1,500 feet to a large tree, each man mounted on a horse, while ropes made "a whistling sound as they were cast over limbs."

What Rummell added to this macabre scene was an instruction supposedly given by the vigilantes that the dance was to continue and no one leave until daylight. The hangings were thus conducted, she reported, to the strains of "The Sunshine of Paradise (V)alley" from Pat's fiddle.

She also added, "After the lynchers left Pat's they visited the home of three brothers who were also prominent members of the gang. They found the three at home, covered them, and without further ado, hanged the two eldest to a live oak tree ... Not wishing to wipe out the family name entirely, they gave the youngest, a boy of 16, strict orders to leave town at once."

This may have been a rather garbled account of the lynchings that led up to the famous Christmas 1883 shoot-out on the main street of McDade. On that Christmas Eve, two brothers were hanged by the vigilantes (no third brother was present to be spared). The event occurred when eight vigilantes entered the Nash Brothers' Rock Front Saloon in McDade and took three men out, including the McLemore brothers, Thad and Wright, and a third man named Henry Pfeiffer. Again, no word was spoken. The three were disarmed, their hands tied behind them, and they were nudged out the door with gun barrels. They were hanged a short way out of town.

As might be expected, the sight of three comrades hanging on the tree Christmas morning riled other Notch Cutters to the killing point. Six of them, all related in one way or another, rode into McDade feeling extremely murderous. Two suspected vigilantes were also in town — Thomas P. Bishop and George Milton — partners in ranching and both owners of local businesses. They were with a third man, probably the local doctor, as Bishop's son records the incident.

The sequence of events during the gun battle varies, but it lasted only a few minutes at midmorning. When the dust settled, both Bishop and Milton were still on their feet. The role of the doctor in the fight, if any, is not reported, but he was not listed among the casualties. Of the outlaws, two were killed outright and four wounded, one of which died the next day.

The three lynched the night before and the two who died in the gunfight were laid out in plain sight of passengers on the noonday train bound for Austin. Whether intended or not, the grisly display made quite an impression on a number of yuletide travelers.

In the wake of this event, several more Notch Cutters packed it in and left the country. Except for periodic flare-ups lasting as long as the hatreds engendered, the reign of the Notch Cutters ended for all intents and purposes on that Christmas morning.

As grim as the tactics of these vigilantes were, they can be counted among the "good guys" — unlike the vigilantes of San Saba County, who got the bit between their teeth and ran amok for ten years (requiring a company of Texas Rangers to finally call a halt).

Vigilantes were a mixed blessing, to say the least. Generally speaking, though, most committee members were more than ready to hang it up when the job was done.

Being a civic-minded vigilante was no bed of roses. Hated, hunted, and often weighed down with "Ox-Bow" memories of killing an innocent person in the heat of the moment, few if any of these long-gone committeemen would ever want historical recognition for their part in the drama.

Jerry Scott's saloon in Lampasas was the scene of more than one shooting involving the Horrells, in one of which Merritt Horrell was shot down without warning.

Fightin' Family

Whether the Horrell brothers of Lampasas were more sinned against than sinners is still open to debate; that they were tough, hard, gutsy gunfighters when aroused is pure fact.

Although best known for the bloody Horrell-Higgins Feud in Lampasas, they also left a lasting impression on New Mexico with what became known as the "Harrold War" — the name misspelled, but the group the same. This was staged on the same ground as the Lincoln County War starring Billy the Kid, which followed a few years later.

Brothers Mart, Tom, Merritt, Ben, and Sam, along with kith and kin, packed nearly all of the action into the years 1873 to 1878. And, of the brothers, only Sam survived. Another brother died violently prior to 1873 in New Mexico.

Described as dark men with solid, powerful bodies, the Horrells were well known for their gun skills but generally were well liked and agreeable. Their various family ranches were scattered north and east of the town of Lampasas along Little Lucy Creek and the Lampasas River.

They may have had a bit of trouble distinguishing their cows from their neighbors. At least one of the neighbors, John

Pinckney Calhoun "Pink" Higgins — tough as any Horrell — was personally convinced of this failing. Both the Horrells and the Higginses had lived in the area from before the Civil War and had been friends until the 1870s, when the question of rustling came up.

In 1873, Capt. Thomas Williams and seven other state police arrived to straighten out the growing problem. Williams had good intentions, but ended up on the road that's paved with them.

The captain started his reform movement in Jerry Scott's saloon on the northwest corner of the Lampasas square. Williams may have been drunk, as reported one teamster he stopped on the road en route. This could account for his attempting to arrest Bill Bowen, a brother-in-law of the Horrells, for wearing a gun into the saloon. Most if not all of the fifteen or so cowboys in the saloon were wearing guns, including a number of Horrells and their friends.

Mart Horrell apparently told Bowen he hadn't done anything wrong, and if he didn't want to be arrested he didn't have to be.

According to C. L. Sonnichsen in *I'll Die Before I'll Run*, there are two versions of what followed this comment: one being, "... Williams grappled with Bowen for the pistol and was fired on by the Horrells" and the other "... as soon as Mart Horrell spoke, Williams drew like a flash and shot Mart, after which the firing became general."

Nevertheless, when the smoke cleared, four state policemen, including Captain Williams, lay dead. Mart Horrell was badly wounded but was taken to the Georgetown jail anyway. As soon as he was well enough to ride, his brothers broke him out.

Having worn out their welcome in Lampasas County, the whole clan sold everything they couldn't carry and headed west. They sent word of their route to the sheriff, just in case he might like to try his hand at stopping them. He didn't care to. The Central Texans were just as glad to see them go.

The Horrells settled in the Ruidoso country west of Roswell, New Mexico, and immediately stirred the natives up.

Listed in *A Directory of New Mexico Desperadoes,* compiled by Peter Hertzog in 1965, the most graphic notation states, "Harrold, Benjamin — One of five brothers from Lampasas County, Texas, whose killing while resisting arrest started an earlier Lincoln County War."

Ben and his brother-in-law Ben Turner were killed in Lincoln during the latter part of 1873, but exactly what sparked the quarrel with the deputy sheriff isn't clear.

The Horrells' side of the story, which they never found an opportunity to give in New Mexico, had nothing to do with "resisting arrest" but involved an attempt to rob them of gold received when selling out in Texas.

Regardless, the New Mexicans had made a mistake. The Horrells' retaliation was swift and without regard to the inappropriateness of the occasion. On December 20, 1873, the Texans burst into a wedding dance in Placitas, killing four men and wounding two.

Apparently, the deputy sheriff was among the four dead. The *Handbook of Texas* says not less than seventeen died before the Horrells got back across the border into Texas. (There are other versions of the swiftness of the Horrells' retaliation, one of which says Ben was killed at the dance, with the brothers arriving immediately afterwards, killing seven Mexicans and one woman. Turner was killed later.)

Whatever the case, New Mexico offered a dead-or-alive reward of $500 for all of the remaining Horrell brothers or $100 for any one of them. A posse of some sixty men rode out to collect, waging a daylong bombardment of the Horrell ranch but causing no damage on either side.

William A. Kerleher, in *Violence in Lincoln County 1869–1881,* notes during January 1874 the president of the United States was petitioned to send in federal troops to quell the disturbance.

But the Horrells were through with New Mexico. Their

future in the state had become very precarious. But, unlike the sigh of relief the Texans had given upon their departure from Lampasas County, the New Mexicans chased them all the way to Fort Davis in the Big Bend, requiring them to fight every step of the way.

Word they were returning, which they may have sent themselves, preceded them to Lampasas. A reception committee met them at the county line in February 1874 bent on discouraging their resettlement in the area. It is said the Horrells did not return the fire, hoping to make a good impression. If this was the case, they failed.

The "prodigal sons" stayed anyway, settling down in ranching southwest of Lampasas on Sulfur Creek just inside the Burnet County line.

And within two years, they had the Higgins faction mad enough to shoot on sight — the problem remaining one of missing cows.

With little regard for sportsmanship, Pink Higgins on January 22, 1877, walked into Jerry Scott's saloon and shot Merritt Horrell down without warning. Some say he shot Merritt in the back as he sat unarmed at the bar.

A little over a month later, the Higgins bunch struck again, bushwhacking Tom and Mart Horrell when they paused at a creek crossing (later called Battle Creek) to let their horses drink.

Tom was shot out of the saddle, but a wounded Mart was able to get his crazed horse under control, dismount, and single handedly run the Higgins bunch off. Tom recovered.

On June 12, 1877, the two factions chanced to meet on the streets of Lampasas and started blazing away at each other, which resulted in the Higgins faction losing one noncombatant brother-in-law and the wounding of one of their partisan fighter friends.

The local citizens had seen enough. They sent for the Texas Rangers and got the best, Maj. John B. Jones, chief of the Frontier Battalion of Texas Rangers. He managed to get both sides to sign peace agreements — a coup no one but Jones thought possible.

Said to be still on file in the adjutant general's office, the double documents agree to regard the feud as "a by gone thing." The truce became famous as the only such agreement ever honored by the feuding factions involved.

So ended that fight, but not the problems for the Horrells.

Both Mart and Tom, accused of a killing not in their style, were shot down by masked men in the Meridian jail December 15, 1878.

Sonnichsen says, while Tom tried to dodge the bullets, "Mart took hold of the bars of the cell door and cursed the mob for the cowards and murderers they were . . . he fell dead, but he didn't need to be ashamed of his exit."

That's as good an epitaph for the Horrell brothers as any.

Sitting in a silver-studded Dick Haye saddle during the days when McNelly's Rangers were cleaning up the Nueces Strip was a death warrant.

Empty Saddles

During the turbulent days in the Nueces Strip, forking a fancy, silver-studded Dick Heye saddle could get a man killed by any "McNelly" who spotted him.

McNellys, sometimes calling themselves Little McNellys, were thirty tough, hard-riding, fast-shooting Texas Rangers who worshiped their sickly, frail, soft-spoken captain, Leander H. McNelly. Long after he was gone, the bond held. Any of them would proudly point out, "Sure, I'm a McNelly."

It was a distinction. The McNellys brought law and order to the Nueces Strip the hard way. It was a brutal "no holds barred" clean-up.

This strip of land is that lying between the Nueces River and the Rio Grande, spotted at the gulf between Corpus Christi and Brownsville on the southern tip of Texas.

By 1875, when McNelly's rangers arrived, an estimated 2,000 ranchers and other citizens had been killed and more than 900,000 head of stock had been stolen by bandit raids, mostly out of Mexico. After other lawful methods had failed, Governor Richard Coke sent McNelly in to straighten out the mess. This unimposing figure had already made his mark as a Confederate soldier and even as a member of the hated state police during Reconstruction. Pound for pound (no more than 135 pounds in all), McNelly was about as deadly and fearless a fighter as Texas ever produced.

Educated for the Methodist ministry, McNelly at age thirty-one — married with two children — was dying of tuberculosis when he took on the job in the Rio Grande Valley. Often mistaken for a preacher, the gentle-looking man with the soft, brown hair and beard, an unlit black cigar between his lips, was, in fact, as ruthless as any man who lacks the restraining handicap of doubt. And McNelly immediately set the tone of his campaign with orders relating to the expensive, well-made, distinctively decorated Dick Heye saddle.

Upon arriving in Corpus Christi the latter part of March 1875, en route to Brownsville, McNelly was informed that eighteen of the silver concho-studded saddles had been stolen in a raid at the Tom Noakes store in a nearby community. Martha Noakes, the wife, had been badly treated.

McNelly ordered the rangers "to empty those saddles on sight. No palavering with riders. Empty them. Leave the men where you drop them and bring the saddles to camp."

George Durham, the ranger who later told of this incident to a writer, Clyde Wantland, also noted that the McNellys, in addition to pistols, carried heavy, one-shot, Sharp carbines, usually reserved for hunting buffalo but preferred by McNelly for their longer range.

The captain was out to make a lasting impression, and he did.

Outlawry and rustling had been brought to a state of near perfection in the lower Rio Grande Valley by a tough little Mexican *hombre* named Juan M. Cordenas, whose family had once owned a good deal of Texas real estate under a Spanish grant. His army of *Cordenistas banditos* and rustlers controlled the strip as far upriver as Laredo, at which point King Fisher, with his rustling operation, more or less took over.

By 1875, Cordenas had built up a very lucrative business in stolen Texas stock, most of which he sold under contract to

Cuba. He, like other Mexicans on both sides of the border, felt Mexico had been rooked out of the Nueces Strip as well as individual parcels of land within it. In some cases they were right. Cordenas himself referred to the rustled cattle as "mama's cows."

With Cordenas, however, it wasn't so much the principle of the thing as the power, political clout, and wealth the stolen stock brought him. And, as undisputed leader of the rustlers, his *Cordenistas* pretty much had the lower Rio Grande Valley "treed" by 1875. Although Cordenas's mother still owned a ranch near Brownsville, he was running the show from Matamoros, Mexico.

Among the many Texas brands burned on the flanks of cattle crossing into Mexico was the Running W of the Kings' Santa Gertrudis ranch. During these years, this famous ranch maintained a twenty-four-hour watch from the top of a tall tower at the headquarters house for any approaching raiders. When McNelly arrived, the owner, Richard King, saw to it that every man in his command was mounted on a good horse, free of charge.

Prior to NcNelly being sent in, other rangers, law enforcement agencies, and even the U.S. Army had made a try at bringing a bit of law and order to the strip — with no luck. Captured outlaws brought in for trial had generally been let go for lack of evidence, as one writer put it, "before the arresting lawmen could water their horses."

McNelly, while warning all other would-be law enforcers to back-off, overcame the handicap of his predecessors by simply not taking any prisoners. No suspected rustlers or bandits were arrested to subsequently be released for lack of evidence.

The outlaws soon realized they were up against a ranger unit as tough and ruthless as they were themselves. Not only riders on Dick Heye saddles, but any passing stranger suspected of working with the *banditos* were in real trouble — and that meant just about any Mexican riding a horse.

McNelly's system for getting information from captured suspected outlaws was very effective — crude, but effective.

Such an unlucky man would be encouraged to tell all he knew about the raiders' plans by being yanked up and down by the neck in hangman fashion, though not quite hard enough to break his neck or completely strangle him. After the information was obtained, he would be hanged for real. If, of course, the man proved to be a law-abiding citizen, he was released. (At just what point such a determination would be made isn't clear.)

McNelly's methods not only upset the outlaws but horrified a good many law-abiding citizens.

His first major clash with the *Cordenistas* came in a fight at Palo Alto, where the McNellys managed to corner a large group of suspected rustlers. The rangers fanned out in skirmish line behind McNelly, walking their horses through a muggy marsh while bullets spatted around them. Not a gun was lifted by a ranger until McNelly signaled the fight was on by firing his own gun.

Only one or two of their targets escaped. One ranger, a sixteen-year-old, was killed and later given a fine funeral.

McNelly incensed the people of Brownsville, most of whom were Mexican, by having the bodies of those killed at Palo Alto displayed in the plaza. Several turned out to be prominent citizens of the town. The bodies were not released to the families until after the ranger's funeral.

McNelly topped this incident, however, by invading Mexico. Some 250 head of cattle had slipped through his fingers and been driven across the Rio Grande near the Mexican community of Las Cuevas, and McNelly wanted them back. Despite telegrams from Washington warning him to stay on the north side of the river, McNelly and his men crossed on a foggy morning — afoot. The federal government had also sent word to the American army garrison stationed at Las Cuevas to render no aid to McNelly if he did cross.

The rustlers, expecting no trouble, were stopping over in

a small community a mile or so south of the river. The McNellys entered the community, captured two of the bandit leaders, and headed back to the river with them before the Mexicans realized what was going on. During the retreat, a number of the Mexicans were killed, but no rangers were hit.

By the time they reached the river, however, the Mexicans were mounted and well organized. Fortunately, just as they were about to overrun the rangers, a young infantry gunner on the Texas side disobeyed orders and opened up with a Gatling gun, killing some thirty Mexicans. It saved the McNellys. Later the noncom explained to superiors his action was "in order to keep the fight from spreading to Texas." He got busted anyway.

In the meantime, McNelly traded his hostages for the rustled cattle. The Mexicans, not realizing the number of cows required, drove 400 head of stolen stock back across the river.

The power of the *Cordenistas* had been broken.

McNelly went on to tackle King Fisher, but by this time the ranger's claws had been drawn. He had to "go by the book" and bring the culprits in. Although he arrested Fisher, the courts let him go for "lack of evidence."

Even so, word had spread upriver that McNelly wasn't to be trifled with and the day of wholesale rustling, robbery, and murder in the Nueces Strip came to an end.

As for those eighteen Dick Heye saddles stolen from Tom Noakes: the McNellys recovered twenty-six.

When Scott Cooley heard about Pete Bader killing a defenseless wounded man and cutting off his finger to obtain his victim's ring, the Mason County War got even hotter.

Another "Kid"

Scott Cooley was as near to being a Texan version of Billy the Kid as makes no difference. Yet, who ever heard of Scott Cooley and who hasn't heard of Billy the Kid?

Even so, their stories are uncannily alike.

Scott, a former Texas Ranger, was embroiled in the Mason County War in Texas during 1875, while Billy took the warpath in 1877 in New Mexico's Lincoln County War.

Neither young man started the feuds in which they fought, just fed the flames. But their reasons for doing so were identical — both were out to avenge a friend and employer's murder. In Cooley's case, it was a former employer, Mason County rancher Tim Williamson. In Billy's, it was a current employer, Lincoln County rancher John Tunstall.

The deaths of the two ranchers caused both situations to boil over, hot enough to turn feuds into guerrilla wars.

Many versions of the Mason County War (also called the Hoo-Doo War) have been written, but all agree that widespread cattle rustling was a basic cause.

In addition to just running off a few of the neighbors' cows, the problem also involved the predominantly German farmers and ranchers with small herds who were losing their cows during the spring roundups. These gathers involved stock from ranches as far north as the Red River that had drifted south during the winter.

A brand inspector, along with representatives from all the ranches, generally kept the ownerships separate — but not always when the owner had few cows to defend. These huge roundups were held just prior to the long trail drives to northern markets held during the summer.

By 1875 the situation was at a dangerous level. A sheriff, John Clark, elected to bring the cow thefts under control, was at best a weak man and at worst as big a villain as any that could be found in or out of the county. Most of the Germans were unaware of his caliber and allied themselves with him.

The festering feud, which many felt was Germans against Texans, exploded on the night of February 18, 1875, following the arrest of nine rustlers who apparently were caught in the act. Four escaped, and a mob took the remaining five from the jail. (These vigilantes were the "Hoo-Doos," a term used to denote those who took the law into their own hands while attempting to keep their own identities secret.)

Making a show to stop the lynchings, the sheriff led a posse (all but himself on foot) and actually overtook the mob in the process of hanging their victims. Hearing the posse coming, the vigilantes shot one man and another escaped. Of the three already hanged, one was cut down in time to save his life.

Three dead and at least ten more to go — the war had started without Cooley. In fact, he wouldn't have gotten involved over a few lynchings, which were common in that day.

Cooley, who had left the employ of his friend Williamson, was working elsewhere at the time. Williamson was not a professional rustler, although he had been for some time out on bond for stealing a beef steer. This was not considered very serious; many fairly honest ranchers ate other men's beef. But for Cooley, the fight soon got personal.

While residents of Mason were upset over the lynchings,

tempers appeared to cool with only a small flare-up. This occurred when a local rancher heard he was next on the list to be strung up, after first being arrested. He promptly rode to town with some sixty friends and relatives at his back and was assured by the sheriff (who had personal reasons for wanting him out of the way) that the rumor was unfounded.

Sheriff Clark then turned his attention to someone he could handle and with whom he had an old grudge, Tim Williamson — Cooley's friend and former employer.

He sent his deputy John Wohrie to bring the young rancher in to Mason. On the way to Mason, the vigilantes waylaid the two. Unarmed, Williamson's only chance of escape was to make a run for it, but Wohrie shot his horse as the mob approached. Williamson died on foot and unarmed, riddled with bullets. Again, no arrests were made.

Cooley rode into Mason shortly after the news reached him. He was heavily armed and as dangerous as he looked. But he lay low for a few days to find out for himself what had happened and who was to blame. He soon came up with his own list.

For some reason he skipped the sheriff immediately and put the deputy sheriff who had arrested Williamson on top. Shooting a man's horse probably cinched it. Cooley went hunting the deputy and found him busy digging a well. After asking his name to be sure, Cooley shot him dead on the spot and scalped him — a gruesome warning to all that Cooley meant business.

Apparently, the sheriff took this news rather nervously. Most of the local people had deserted him after the lynchings. To get their support back, Clark concocted a story that Cooley and his men planned to attack Mason itself. The citizens rallied to the defense of their town and followed Clark out to a point where Cooley was expected to pass on his way to Mason.

In the meantime, perhaps to furnish targets for the defenders, the sheriff had sent a message to two other young ranchers that they were wanted in Mason. Having no reason to fear an ambush, and not being under any suspicion of rustling, the two saddled up and headed for town in one another's company.

When they came to the spot where the sheriff's "posse" was waiting to intercept Cooley's gang, the young ranchers were shot off their horses by a barrage of fire from the sheriff and his inner circle. This was done much to the horror of most of the citizens present.

One of the wounded ranchers survived, thanks to help from a member of the posse, but the other was finished off.

This took place almost under the noses of the Texas Rangers who arrived in the county as this one-sided battle was going on. Some of the local citizens had petitioned the governor for help, and Maj. John B. Jones, commander of all the Frontier Battalion (composed of about thirty ranger companies), arrived. The major brought along Company D, unknowingly having picked Cooley's old company.

While the rangers settled in to find out what was going on, Cooley and his group proceeded to even the score. The ambush of the two ranchers and killing of one of them while he lay helpless on the ground brought even more friends from as far away as San Antonio to ride with Cooley.

Cooley, having gotten the story of what happened from the survivor, immediately added more names to his list. He rode up to the home of Karl Bader in neighboring Llano County and gunned him down. Perhaps this was a mistake, as it was Bader's brother Pete credited with the actual killing of the wounded man and cutting off his finger to obtain his victim's ring.

Cooley and several others then set up an ambush in Mason to take care of the sheriff and any others of his group they could. The sheriff slipped out of town, but three of his associates faced the fire. One, the official brand inspector, credited with being hand-and-glove with Clark (although one writer strongly disputes this), was shot off his horse without warning. None of the others on either side were seriously wounded.

In the meantime, the rangers had gone into action — but for once with little or no results. When sent out to arrest Cooley and his associates, they came back empty-handed — "couldn't find him."

It took their commander very little time to find out what the difficulty was — not in finding him, but in arresting him when they did. According to ranger James B. Gillett's account, some of Cooley's former buddies not only found him but told him they didn't care "how many Dutchmen he killed."

However, Major Jones did not share in the "good ol' buddy," philosophy and, says Gillett, he lined up the men of Company D and gave them the option of shaping up or quitting the rangers. Some did quit.

Arrests did pick up after that, but Cooley wasn't among the captured in Mason County. He was jailed about that time in Lampasas County, where he may have been lying low. He had only a brief stay in the Lampasas jail before his friends had him out. Gillett was apparently never aware Cooley was taken out of circulation while the rangers were looking for him.

Meanwhile, matters in Mason County eased off and the rangers left. But the war wasn't over yet. Pete Bader finally got what many felt was overdue on January 20, 1876, when he was killed and scalped. This happened while Cooley was in jail but certainly it would carry his approval.

By this time Sheriff Clark had resigned and disappeared over the horizon, with Cooley not far behind. Whether the young cowboy was actually on the trail of the man he felt most responsible for his friend Williamson's death is not known for sure. But they were destined not to meet. All indications point to Cooley dying shortly after leaving Mason, either by being poisoned or of an illness.

Whatever the case, the Mason County War was over. The *Handbook of Texas* notes: "No trial in Mason County ever convicted any man of either faction for any of the murders... Not until after 1876 did the county settle down to respectable peace, law, and order."

For Cooley the end would have been anticlimactic, to say the least. Unlike Billy the Kid, who ended up being shot in the dark by a former riding buddy, Pat Garret, Cooley's end was neither as dramatic nor as well documented.

One version even ends on a happier note: Cooley, it says, rode west and settled in Arizona, where he lived out a long and peaceful life.

What is known for sure is that, of the two wild cowboys whose personal vendettas played havoc in two county wars, the legend of Billy the Kid lives on — while Scott Cooley rode off into oblivion.

Charles H. Howard had few, if any, scruples — but he knew how to die. Fearlessly facing a horde of maddened Mexicans intent on executing him, he called out the command, "Fire!"

Pepper Hot Salt War

The El Paso Salt War can only be described as a battle among scoundrels. There were no "good guys."
 It all started when someone discovered that the salt beds (called salt lakes) in arid country about 110 miles east of El Paso (then Franklin) were being worked for a small profit by the poor Mexican peons living on both sides of the Rio Grande river border. Using ox-drawn wagons, the Mexicans would load up with the salt and take it to the interior of Mexico and sell it.
 Money could be made by charging these Mexicans a fee. But first, ownership of the salt had to be acquired.
 By the time it was all over in 1877, the former ruling Republican party in El Paso County was in ruins, the U.S. Army's reputation tarnished, the Texas Rangers' record blotted, and the sanctity of the Catholic Church clergy considerably shaken up.
 On the other hand, for pure guts, greed and double-cross, the story can't be beat.
 While others were involved with the project at the start, it boiled down to one American *gringo* and his cohorts on the

one hand, and a couple of Machiavellian Italians (one a Catholic priest) on the other.

It began as a legal, if not strictly above-board, business deal among a group of Republican businessmen in the late 1860s. Their party controlled the county, having no problems until salt became an issue.

The Mexican vote — the vast majority — was controlled by two Italians, Don Louis Cardis, an American lawyer, and Fr. Antonio Borrajo, a Catholic parish priest whose church was at the village of San Elizario, downriver from El Paso. This community was the starting point for the salt caravans.

Both Cardis and Borrajo had unlimited influence upon the Mexican voters, who outnumbered the whites by at least fifty to one.

Historian Walter Prescott Webb said of Borrajo: "This Italian . . . wove in and out of the shadows like an evil spirit transplanted from the age of the Medicis."

And Cardis, except for being a personal coward, wasn't much better. He was the political boss of the region, and had blocked an earlier attempt to secure the salt deposits for the people of El Paso.

Fr. Borrajo, whose influence over his flock even exceeded that of Cardis, expected, in exchange for his influence, to be given a half share in the salt, along with several other concessions. If he received what he wanted, the *padre* agreed to tell the Mexicans to pay whatever fee was charged for the salt. What Cardis expected as his cut is a bit vague.

At any rate, the Republicans wouldn't deal, and in fact, had already fallen out among themselves, splintering into the Salt Ring and Anti-Salt Ring factions. None of them got any salt and simply destroyed the Republican power in El Paso County.

It probably was over anyway, for when the *padre* and Cardis found out the Republicans weren't going to cut them in on the salt deal they backed a Democrat, Charles H. Howard, for district judge (his Republican predecessor had been murdered during the salt dispute). Howard was a man of undoubted courage, an excellent pistol shot, a man with no known scruples.

Apparently with his fingers crossed, Howard promised Fr. Borrajo and Cardis whatever they wanted. In the same election that put Howard on the bench, Cardis was elected state representative.

Before his two "partners" knew what was up, Howard double-crossed them both by filing a private claim for the salt in the name of his father-in-law. (Some of the salt deposits already belonged to Sam Maverick of San Antonio, but for unknown reasons neither he nor his salt figured into the Salt War story.)

At any rate, as soon as it became obvious that Howard wasn't about to share his salt, all hell broke loose.

Fr. Borrajo roused the Mexicans on both sides of the river into a frenzy. His tactics were so "unfatherly" that his bishop tried to remove him from the San Elizario church, but failed. Not only did Fr. Borrajo defy his spiritual leader, but he informed his parishioners the bishop was a Protestant and he and his priests were a bunch of thieves.

Meanwhile, Cardis returned from the state legislature and set about undermining Howard's position with the voters, which wasn't very difficult. The judge responded to this by publicly pistol whipping Cardis on more than one occasion. Cardis never would attempt to defend himself, and Howard finally lost patience and shot him dead.

With this action, the Mexicans really went after the judge's blood, causing Howard to make a short stay in New Mexico before returning to the fray. When he got back, he continued to upset the Mexicans, causing another Catholic priest, Fr. Bourgade, to rescue him from an infuriated mob.

Even this wouldn't have been possible without Howard's promise to leave Texas. His friends put up a $12,000 bond as assurance against his ever coming back.

However, Howard had hardly settled down again in New

Mexico when word came that his old enemy Fr. Borrajo — who had finally moved across the river into Mexico — had encouraged the Mexicans to send a wagon train to pick up as much of Howard's salt as they wanted, free of charge.

Enraged, Howard managed to get the legal papers necessary to claim the salt for himself when the loaded wagons arrived back in San Elizario. Along with two business friends — John Atkinson, his bondsman, and John McBride — Howard returned to Texas to collect his salt or the price for it.

He had squeaked through so many dangerous confrontations with the Mexicans, he apparently felt he could again. He was wrong.

However, knowing there would be trouble, Howard had his bondsman bring along $11,000, hoping to cover the $12,000 bond, in case of need. He also collected a company of newly recruited Texas Rangers under the command of Lt. John B. Tays to go with him to their headquarters in San Elizario.

Tays, whom Howard earlier had described as "a good man, but very slow," in turn sent for Capt. Thomas Blair at Franklin (El Paso) to bring regular U.S. troops to his assistance. Blair did arrive with some fourteen men when the Mexicans had Howard and his party cornered in the rangers' quarters at San Elizario.

The mob, made up mostly of Mexican nationals, was led by Chico Barela, who managed to scare the army captain into hightailing it back to El Paso. Whatever justification the military commander might have felt he had for this action, "his conduct certainly can never stir in his descendants much ancestral pride," Webb points out.

Protected by the rangers and the thick adobe walls of their headquarters in San Elizario, Howard and his two friends, John Atkinson and John McBride, should have been able to withstand the siege of the mob at least until help arrived.

However, after a week or more — with one ranger killed

and at least one friend of Howard's, a shopkeeper in the town, brutally murdered — and no help in sight, the fatal mistake was made. Lieutenant Tays agreed to come out and parley with the Mexicans.

As Webb again points out, "It is an axiom in Texas history that when a Texan fights a Mexican he can win; when he parleys he is doomed . . ."

This turned out to be the case. Howard thought he might be able to save the others by turning himself over to the mob, and went with Tays to parley. The Mexicans promptly cut them off from any retreat back to the building.

All Tays managed in his negotiations was achieving the distinction of being the first and only Texas Ranger ever to surrender his command or hand over others to a mob. With all the shortcomings in their conduct at various times, a Texas Ranger had never been known to back up under any provocation.

James B. Gillett, a ranger at the time (who didn't arrive in El Paso until some weeks later), wrote that the rangers under Tays were "furious at this surrender," one of the youngest of them yelling at his commander: "The only difference between you and a skunk is that the skunk has a white streak down his back."

Chico Barela, however, did make a deal to spare the lives of Howard and his friends for the $11,000 Atkinson had brought along. Barela may have intended to keep his word, but Fr. Borrajo sent a message to "Shoot all the gringos and I will absolve you."

The best the Mexican commander could do was save the lives of the Texas Rangers. Howard, Atkinson, and McBride were killed — executed one at a time.

Howard, shot first, walked erect with his hands behind him before turning to face the mob, calling out in broken Spanish that they were about to execute 300 men. Then, slapping his chest, he shouted, "Fire!"

Atkinson, the next to go, also gave the command to fire.

Details of McBride's execution aren't given, other than indicating that he, too, died bravely.

Disarmed, the rangers departed safely, while the mob turned their attention to sacking the town and hauling everything they could across the river into Mexico.

Most of the Mexicans remaining in San Elizario had taken little or no part in the uprising and naturally felt they had nothing to worry about. A bad miscalculation.

Within days, the army, along with rangers and various other white men, were back in San Elizario wreaking vengeance upon any Mexican they could lay hands on. Most of the guilty were safely across the border in Mexico.

It was a sordid ending to a sordid mess.

No one had won the war. Some participants had paid with their lives; others, such as Fr. Borrajo, simply faded out of the picture, possibly into the interior of Mexico.

Despite putting on a very poor show, the army came out a winner in that Fort Bliss, about to be closed that year, became a permanent post.

As for the poor Mexicans trying to scrape out a meager living hauling salt to Mexico — they ended up having to pay for it anyway.

Bell Starr, tough as any man, earned her title as Queen of the Outlaws, but her failures as a mother proved her undoing.

Female of the Species

Bell Starr, tough as any man, made her mark as an "outlaw queen" in both Texas and Oklahoma. Her fatal mistake was whipping up on the wrong kid — her own. But before "junior" brought mama down with two blasts of a shotgun, Bell Starr called her own shots.

During the 1870s and '80s, Bell made a niche for herself in outlaw annals on both sides of the river.

About 5'4" tall, weighing around 135, dark hair and eyes, Bell added up to being as homely as a mud fence in a rain storm. Even so, she must have been quite a gal — making up in personality what she lacked in looks.

She certainly had male admirers, although her taste in men ran to outlaws, Indians, and a combination of both. During her career she had innumerable lovers and two husbands at different times.

Her first recorded lover was the outlaw Cole Younger, who, along with his brothers, rode with the James boys. Although he failed to marry Bell despite fathering her oldest child, Pearl, Bell never seemed to hold it against him. She then married a horse thief, Jim Reed, who fathered her son Eddie. Shortly thereafter, Jim was killed while resisting arrest, and Bell moved on to Blue Duck, an Indian with whom she had her picture taken but acquired no marriage license.

Following this affair she married a Cherokee Indian, Sam Starr, and adopted the surname by which she is known. After Starr was shot to death, she took up with a half-breed Bill July. There may have been other men in her life, but these were the most visible.

One male she couldn't control was her son Eddie, who ran wild, but not apparently on order. With an example like Bell, it's little wonder he turned out very much like her. Unfortunately, on her death bed only her daughter heard Bell name Eddie as the culprit. Pearl protected him with the result that the cause of death February 3, 1889, was listed officially as death by gunshot at the hands of an "unknown assailant."

It was pretty obvious, however, to at least two of her friends that Eddie was the murderer. The friends, J. F. Short and Dr. Jesse Mooney, independently came to this conclusion.

The murder took place shortly after Bell had chastised Eddie for taking her horse — with the result, said Short, "Reed's face looked as though it might have been run through a meat chopper . . . I met young Reed in a little town called Broken, 12 miles from Bell's home . . . I asked him how it happened that he had been so badly beaten about the face. He said 'Lady Jinks [the name he called his mother] worked my head over with a quirt handle . . . [and added] I'm going to get even and someone is going to get killed.'"

Apparently, Bell had been upset with her son for taking her favorite horse for a ride. Had he stolen someone else's horse, Bell would have been considerably more tolerant.

But the attack on her son proved to be the last violent act of the "queen's" career, culminating a long list of misdeeds she had survived.

On at least one other occasion she had been shot, but the man who did it didn't live to tell the tale.

According to Dr. Mooney, the year before she was killed he was called to attend her — riding ninety miles over back trails, avoiding main roads. In two days the doctor and messenger arrived at a hideout cave known as Starr Dugout and Spring, located in the Choctaw Nation. The large cave was set in the side of a small mountain.

Bell Starr was lying wounded on an Indian blanket on the dirt floor. She had been shot in the upper left shoulder, the bullet still embedded. While later noting how stoic and brave she was, the doctor never mentioned the events leading to her condition, if, in fact, anyone ever told him.

However, Bell is quoted as saying, "I don't want you to say nothin' 'bout me gettin' hit to nobody. Somebody else might try it if they hear 'bout this. The one that done it won't ever be doin' no more talkin'."

During their fairly short marriage, Sam Starr and Bell both did federal time for horse stealing. They also stole the life savings of an elderly Indian in whose home they were guests. This led to Sam being killed by a cousin who was an Indian policeman.

Bell apparently got her taste for excitement during the Civil War when she was growing up in Missouri. One account says during the last two years of the war she was a spy for the Confederacy.

Born Myra Bell Shirley in Missouri on February 5, 1846, or as her tombstone has it, 1848, she received some formal education before the family moved to Texas after the war.

The Shirleys settled east of Dallas, and the girl known as Myra began calling herself Bell — a prelude to discarding, as it were, any trappings of respectability.

As it turned out, raising children wasn't Bell's strong suit. Pearl became a highly successful prostitute and Eddie a less successful horse thief and murderer. But for Bell, being a well-known outlaw meant reaching her ultimate goal.

While still married to Starr, she received what probably for her was the equivalent of an Oscar for an actress — a price on her head.

All the recognition she ever sought was summed up in an early reward poster:

> REWARD $10,000 in Gold Coin
> Will be paid by the U.S. Government
> for apprehension Dead or Alive
> of Sam and Belle Starr
> Wanted for Robbery, Murder, Treason
> And other Acts Against the Peace
> And Dignity of the U.S. Government
> (signed) Thomas Crail, Major
> 8th Missouri Cavalry Commanding

Those who knew her well would have wondered why "horse thief" had been left out, as this was known to be one of her specialties.

Bell gloried in her reputation as "Queen of the Outlaws" and did her best to live up to the image. She even went to dances wearing her guns, while all the men had to leave them at the door.

Said to be a living terror when riled, the "queen" otherwise was pleasant, docile, and mild-mannered. Bell's log house overlooking the river in a "U" bend named (perhaps for sentimental reasons) "Younger Bend" was headquarters for outlaws either in resident or passing through. She may have controlled a band; certainly she acted as "middleman" in disposing of many stolen horses for her friends.

Said to have a crude sense of humor and a flare for the dramatic, Bell dressed in a flowing black velvet riding habit with two six-shooters hanging on her hips. She rode a large black horse sidesaddle and lived outwardly at any rate as "a lady." According to one report, her home was furnished with a piano, shelves of books, nice rugs, and other items of culture. She was well liked by most of her neighbors and those living in the communities she visited.

But, despite any attempts to appear "ladylike," Bell was no lady. She was as tough a bird as ever rode the "hoot owl trail." A woman who could disfigure her son's face with the handle of her quirt, steal an old man's last cent, and rob and perhaps murder others, Bell could never have made the social register.

Although details of her unsavory career are more circumstantial than substantiated, there's little room to doubt her lawless character.

Bell seemed fond of her daughter Pearl, and despite "occasional differences," she and Eddie had a lot in common. But it would appear the strongest bond within the family was between Pearl and her younger brother. She not only shielded him from the consequences of murdering his mother, but is said to have turned later to prostitution to raise money to get him out of jail. This proved to be a highly successful career for her, as she was well known as the "daughter of the famous Bell Starr, Queen of the Outlaws."

After Eddie's death in a gun fight, Pearl confirmed the doctor's suspicions. The two met again at Eddie's funeral and Pearl told Dr. Mooney that just before her mother died, "She opened her eyes after we got her home in bed, and she whispered to me, 'Baby — your brother Eddie shot me — I turned and seen him before he cracked down the second time.'"

Her funeral followed with the body lying on an Indian blanket in a plain pine board box. Her arms were crossed and her right hand held her favorite pearl-handled .45. The Cherokee pallbearers then placed the lid back on the coffin, nailed it shut, and in silence carefully lowered the box into the grave before covering it up.

It had taken a chip-off-the-ole-block to bring down the "Queen of the Outlaws."

Bibliography

Moment of Truth

Jenkins, John Holland. *Recollections of Early Texas*. Austin: University of Texas Press, 1958.
"Plenty of Action at San Jacinto." *Frontier Times*. Vol. 26, No. 12 (September 1949).
Smithwick, Noah. *Evolution of a State*. Reprint of 1900 ed. Austin: University of Texas Press, 1983.
The Texans. Text by David Nevin. *The Wild West,* Time-Life Series. Time-Life Books, 1980.
Webb, Walter Prescott, et. al., eds. *The Handbook of Texas*. 2 vols. Austin: Texas State Historical Association, 1952. 2:554.
Wortham, Louis J. *A History of Texas*. Fort Worth: 1924. 3:295, 437.

Indian Fighter

Affleck, D. "Great Battle of Painted Rock." Reprinted from *El Paso Times. Frontier Times,* January 1924.
Webb, Walter Prescott, et. al., eds. *The Handbook of Texas*. 2 vols. Austin: Texas State Historical Association, 1952. 1:789.
Webb, Walter Prescott. *The Texas Rangers, A Century of Frontier Defense*. 2nd. ed. Austin: University of Texas Press, 1965.

A Bloody Mess

Maverick, Mary A. *Memoirs*. Edited by Rena Maverick Green. San Antonio: Alamo Printing, 1921.
Webb, Walter Prescott, et. al., eds. *The Handbook of Texas*. 2 vols. Austin: Texas State Historical Association, 1952.
Wortham, Louis J. *A History of Texas*. Fort Worth: 1924. 4:65.

Sweet Revenge

Johnson, Frank W. *Texas and Texans*. Chicago and New York: The American Historical Society, 1914. 1:491–493.
Winaki, Norman. "When Lee and Grant Were Allies." *Pioneer West,* Vol. 1, No. 3 (September 1967).
Wortham, Louis J. *A History of Texas*. Fort Worth: 1924. Vol. 4.

Captive Luck

Lee Nelson. *Three Years Among the Comanches*. Norman: University of Oklahoma Press, 1957.

Home Front Atrocities

Branda, Eldon S., ed. *The Handbook of Texas, A Supplement*. Vol. 3. Austin: Texas State Historical Association, 1976. 3:321.
Burnet County History. 2 vols. Burnet, TX: Eakin Press, 1979.
Nichols, James Wilson. *Now You Hear My Horn*. Austin: University of Texas Press, 1967.
100 Years in Bandera, 1853–1953. J. Marvin Hunter, 1953.
Scarbrough, Clara Stearns. *Land of Good Water, A Williamson County Texas History*. Georgetown, TX: Williamson County Sun Publishers, 1973.
Smithwick, Noah. *The Evolution of a State*. Austin: University of Texas Press, 1983. 262–263.

Heel-Flies

Bishop, W. W. *Rise and Fall of Sparta*.
Hunter, John Warren. "Heel Fly Time in Texas." *Frontier Times,* April, May, June, 1924.
Watts, Peter. *A Dictionary of the Old West, 1850–1900*. New York: Alfred A. Knopf, 1977.

Vengeance

"Vengeance on the Frontier." Taken from a book *With the Border Ruffians,* by R. H. Williams, and reprinted in *Frontier Times*, Vol. 26, No. 10 (July 1948).

Two of a Kind

Conversations with C. W. Duncan, Sr., concerning a meeting between Hardin and Duncan's father in 1880s; also with Frank E. Parks, of Killeen, TX, concerning death of Hardin by hand of Parks' kinsman, John Selman, Sr., in El Paso.
Fuller, Henry C. *Adventures of Bill Longley.* Facsimile ed. San Augustine, TX: S. Malone, 1983.
The Gunfighters. Text by Paul Tachtman. *The Wild West,* Time-Life Series. Time-Life Books: 1980.
Tyler, George. *History of Bell County.* 1936. Dayton Kelly, 1966.
Williamson County Sun [Georgetown, TX]. Centennial issue, May 19, 1977.
Wiltsey, Norman B. "Gunfighter." Part 2. *Real West,* November 1968.

Vigilantes

Bishop, Luckett P., Sr. "Shoot-Out on Christmas Day." *Frontier Times,* June/July, 1965.
Martin, G. K. "Land of the Noose — Yegua Knobbs." *Old West,* Spring 1969.
Rummell, Helen. "When Eleven Were Lynched." *Frontier Times,* Vol. 4, No. 10 (July 1930). Reprinted from *Austin American-Statesman.*
Scarbrough, Clara Stearns. *Land of Good Water, A Williamson County History.* Georgetown, TX: Williamson County Sun Publishers, 1973.
Watts, Peter. *A Dictionary of the Old West.* New York: Alfred A. Knopf, 1977.
Webb, Walter Prescott, et. al., eds. *The Handbook of Texas.* 2 vols. Austin: Texas State Historical Association, 1952. 2:842.

Fightin' Family

Gillett, James B. *Six Years With the Texas Rangers.* University of Nebraska Press, 1976.
Hertzog, Peter, comp. *Directory of New Mexican Desperados.* 1965.
Keleher, William A. *Violence in Lincoln County, 1869–1881.* Albuquerque: University of New Mexico Press, 1982.

Sonnichsen. C. L. *I'll Die Before I'll Run*. New York: Harper and Brothers Publishers, 1951.
Webb, Walter Prescott, et. al., eds. *The Handbook of Texas*. Austin: Texas State Historical Association, 1952. 1:836.

Empty Saddles

Durham, George, as told to Clyde Wantland. *Taming of the Nueces Strip, The Story of McNelley's Rangers*. Austin: University of Texas Press, 1962.
Webb, Walter Prescott. "McNelley's Rangers." *True West*, January/February, 1962.

Another "Kid"

Gillett, James B. *Six Years with the Texas Rangers*. Austin: Von Boeckmann-Jones Co., 1921.
Holmes, Mrs. Henry M. *Diary, 1875-1876*. "The Hoo-Doo War Years." Mason, TX: Mason County Historical Commission, 1985.
Hunter, J. Marvin, ed. "Brief History of the Early Days in Mason County." *Frontier Times*, Vol. 6, Nos. 2 and 5 (February and November, 1929); "The Hoo-Doo War in Mason County," Vol. 14, No. 4 (January 1938).
Mason County Communities. Mason, TX: Mason County Sesquicentennial Committee, 1986.
Mason County Historical Book. "Daniel Hoerster and the Mason County War" by Dave Johnson, and "Henry Marcus Holmes, A Texas Law Practice, 1875-1895" by H. L. Warburton, Jr. Mason, TX: Mason County Historical Commission, 1986.
Sonnichsen, C. L. *Ten Texas Feuds*. Albuquerque: University of New Mexico Press, 1957.
Webb, Walter Prescott. *The Texas Rangers, A Century of Frontier Defense*. Austin: University of Texas Press, 1965.

Salt War Disgrace

Gillett, James B. *Six Years with the Texas Rangers*. Austin: Von Boeckmann-Jones, 1921.
Hyatt, Frieda and Samual. "Salt War of Texas." *True West*, September/October, 1956.
Webb, Walter Prescott. *The Texas Rangers, A Century of Frontier Defense*. Austin: University of Texas Press, 1965.

Pepper Hot Salt War

Gillett, James B. *Six Years with the Texas Rangers*. Austin: Von Boeckmann-Jones, 1921.

Hyatt, Frieda and Samual. "Salt War of Texas." *True West*, September/October, 1956.

Webb, Walter Prescott, et. al., eds. *The Handbook of Texas*. 2 vols. Austin: Texas State Historical Association, 1952. 2:536–537.

Webb, Walter Prescott. *The Texas Rangers, A Century of Frontier Defense*. Austin: University of Texas Press, 1965.

Female of the Species

Hendricks, George G. *Badmen of the West*. San Antonio: The Naylor Company, 1950.

Mooney, Charles W. "Bell Starr's Killer Recalled." *True West*, January/February, 1969.

Short, J. F. "Graham Knew Bell Starr and Life in Indian Territory." *Graham Leader Reporter*, April 20, 1972.

Surge, Frank. *Western Lawmen*. Lerner Publications: 1969.

Author Bio

Retired newspaper reporter and columnist GRA'DELLE DUNCAN was a history buff and freelance writer whose books include *Killeen Area Bicentennial Sketch Book, Central Texas Diary, Killeen: Tale of Two Cities,* and *Texas Tough: Dangerous Men in Dangerous Times.*

A graduate of the University of Texas Journalism School (now Communications School), Duncan also published numerous magazine articles on New Mexico and Texas history.

Her roots in Central Texas stem from the 1850s and 1870s, the Duncan branch having arrived during the latter period a couple of jumps ahead of the posse. She passed away in 2004.

Index

A
Aikens, William, 32, 33–34
Alamo, Battle of, 1, 23
Alsup, Wade, 69–70
Anderson, Wilson "Wilsie," 61
Atkinson, John, 96, 97–98
Austin American-Statesman, 69

B
Bader, Karl, 88
  Pete, 88, 89
Baker, Moseley, 3
Bandera, Texas, 41
Barela, Chico, 96, 97
Bastrop County, Texas, 66
Bell County, Texas, 65
Big Bend country, 35
Billy the Kid, 73, 85, 90
Bishop, Luckett P., Sr., 67
  Thomas P., 70–71
Blair, Thomas, 96
Blanco County, Texas, 40
Blue Duck, 102
Borrajo, Antonio, 94, 95–96, 97, 98
Bourgade, Fr., 95
Bowen, Bill, 74
Brownsville, Texas, 82
Brushy Creek, 20
Buena Vista, Battle of, 27
Burnet County, Texas, 38, 39, 76

C
Cameron, Ewen, 26
Camp Verde, 41
captives, of Indians, 17, 20–21, 32–35
Cardis, Don Louis, 94, 95
Chief Isimanicaand, 19
Chiff, Sol, 54
Choctaw Nation, 103
Civil War, 37
Clark, John, 86, 87, 89
Clements brothers, 61–62
Coke, Richard, 79
Comanches, 10–14, 17–21, 32–35
Comanche, Texas, 62
"Come to the Bower," 4
Comfort, Texas, 41
Confederacy, 37, 38, 46, 103
Confederate army, 42, 47, 60
Conner, Captain, 27
Cooley, Scott, 85–90
Cordenas, Juan M., 80–83
Cordenistas, 80–83
Corpus Christi, Texas, 80
Council House Fight, 17–21
Cow Creek, 39

D
Davis Mountains, 32
Dawson, Nicholas M., 23
Dead Man's Hole, 39
Delgado, Pedro, 4–5
Dick Heye saddle, 79, 80, 83

Directory of New Mexico Desperadoes, A, 75
Duff, James E., 41
Durham, George, 80

E
Earhart, Pat, 69
El Paso County, Texas, 93, 94
El Paso Salt War, 93–98
El Paso, Texas, 62
Evolution of a State, The, 5

F
First Texas Volunteers, 25
Fisher, King, 80, 83
Flacco, 9–10
Floyd, Jim, 69–70
  Young, 69–70
Ford, John S. "Rip," 25
Fort Bliss, 98
Fort Davis, 76
forts, 27–28
French, Dick, 53–57
  Jim, 53–57
Frontier Times, 46, 67, 69

G
Gainesville, Great Hanging at, 42
Garret, Pat, 90
Giddings, Texas, 62
Gillespie, R. A., 11, 12, 13, 14
Gillett, James B., 89, 97
Goliad Massacre, 1, 23
Gonzales, 2
Grove Community, 65

H
Handbook of Texas, 75, 89
Hardin, John Wesley, 59–63
Harrison, E. M., 10, 11–12, 13, 14–15
"Harrold War," 73
Hays, John Coffee "Jack," 9–15, 25, 26–27
Henderson, J. Pinckney, 24
Hertzog, Peter, 75

Higgins, John Pinckney Calhoun "Pink," 74, 76
Home Guards, 45–50
"Hoo-Doos," 86
Hoo-Doo War *(see also* Mason County War, 85)
Horrell, Ben, 73, 75
  Mart, 73, 74, 76, 77
  Merritt, 73, 76
  Sam, 73
  Tom, 73, 76, 77
Horrell-Higgins Feud, 73
Houston, Sam, 2–6, 38
Howard, Charles H., 94–96, 97
Huamantla, Mexico, 27
Hubbard, John R., 39
Hubbard Falls, 39
Hunter, J. Marvin, 41, 42
  John Warren, 45–46, 47–50
Hunter's Magazine, 46

I
I'll Die Before I'll Run, 74

J
James boys, 101
Johnson, A. S., 25
Jones, John B., 76–77, 88, 89
July, Bill, 102

K
Kerleher, William A., 75
King, Richard, 81
Knobbs, Texas, 67
Kuykendall, J. H., 2
  John, 69–70

L
LaGrange, Texas, 26
Lampasas County, Texas, 89
Lampasas River, 73
Lampasas, Texas, 73, 76
Lane, Walter P., 26
Las Cuevas, Mexico, 82
Lee, Nelson, 31–35
Lee County, Texas, 66, 69
Leona River, 54

Lincoln County, 85
Lincoln County War, 73, 75, 85
Little Cedar Lick, Tennessee, 10
Little Lucy Creek, 73
Llano County, Texas, 88
Longley, Bill, 59–63
  Cale, 61
Lynch's Ferry, 2

M
McBride, John, 96, 97–98
McCulloch, Ben, 11, 25, 26, 27
McDade, Texas, 67, 69, 70
McDowell, Catherine W., 40
McLemore, Thad, 70
  Wright, 70
McMasters, ———, 39
McNelly, Leander H., 79–83
McNellys, 79
Martin, G. K., 67
Mason County, 85
Mason County War, 85, 89
Mason, Texas, 87, 88
Matamoros, Mexico, 47, 81
Maverick, Mary Adams, 18–19
  Sam, 95
Menefee, John S., 4
Merony, Parson, 65
Mexican War, 10, 23–28
Mexico City, Mexico, 26
Mier expedition, 23, 26
Milton, George, 70–71
Minshull, Asa, 54, 56–57
  Hiram, 54
Mission San Jose de Aguayo, 19
Monterrey, Battle of, 24
Mooney, Jesse, 102–103, 105

N
Nash Brothers' Rock Front Saloon, 70
Nichols, James Wilson, 40
Noakes, Martha, 80
  Tom, 80, 83
Notch Cutters, 66–71
Now You Hear My Horn, 40
Nueces, Battle of the, 41
Nueces Strip, 79, 81

O
Oatmeal Creek, 38
Old West, 67
Olive brothers, 67–68
One Hundred Years in Bandera 1853–1953, 41

P
Painted Rock, 11
Palo Alto, 82
Peace Party Conspiracy, 42
Pfeiffer, Henry, 70
Placitas, New Mexico, 75
Polk, President, 24
Prison of Peote, 27

R
Reconstruction, 60, 80
Redd, Capt., 19
Reed, Eddie, 101, 102–105
  Jim, 101–102
Republican party, 93, 94
Rio Grande Valley, 80, 81
Roswell, New Mexico, 75
Rummell, Helen, 69, 70
rustling, 80, 85

S
Salado, Texas, 26
San Antonio, Texas, 17, 18, 53
San Elizario, 94, 96, 98
San Jacinto, Battle of, 1–6, 10
San Luis Potosi, 26
San Saba County, Texas, 71
Santa Anna, Antonio López de, 2–6, 25, 26, 27
Santa Fe expedition, 23
Santa Gertrudis ranch, 81
Scott, Bake, 69–70
  Jerry, 74, 76
  John R., 38–39

Winfield, 24, 26, 27
Shirley, Myra Bell (see Starr, Bell)
Short, J. F., 102
Smithwick, Noah, 5-6, 39-40
Smithwick, Texas, 39
Sonnichsen, C. L., 74, 77
Starr, Bell, 101-105
  Sam, 102, 103
Starr Dugout and Spring, 103
Sulfur Creek, 76
Sutton-Taylor Feud, 62

T

Taylor, Zachary, 23, 24, 27
Tays, John B., 96-97
Texas, secession of, 37
Texas Rangers, 9-15, 71, 76, 79, 88, 93, 96
Texas Revolution, 1
Texas soldiers, 23-28
Three Years Among the Comanches, 33
Tunstall, John, 85
Turner, Amasa, 5
  Ben, 75
Two Sisters, 2

U

Unionists, 37-42, 47, 49-50
United States Army, 25, 93
Uvalde, Texas, 54

V

vigilantes, 65-71, 86
Violence in Lincoln County 1869-1881, 75

W

Walker, Samuel H., 25, 27
Wantland, Clyde, 80
Webb, Walter Prescott, 94, 96, 97
Webster, Martha, 20
  Mrs., 20-21
Weidemann, Dr., 19-20
Wells, Lysander, 19
Wharton, Col., 5
Wilbarger, J. W., 10
Williams, R. H., 54-57
  Thomas, 74
Williamson, Tim, 85, 86, 87
Williamson County, Texas, 41, 66, 68
With the Border Ruffians, 54
Wohrie, John, 87

Y

Yegua Creek, 66, 67
Younger, Cole, 101
  Pearl, 101, 102, 103, 105
Younger Bend, 104

www.ingramcontent.com/pod-product-compliance
Lightning Source LLC
Chambersburg PA
CBHW070203100426
42743CB00013B/3029